I0103628

Sidney Colvin

Guide to the Exhibition of Chinese and Japanese Paintings in the Print and Drawing Gallery

Sidney Colvin

Guide to the Exhibition of Chinese and Japanese Paintings in the Print and Drawing Gallery

ISBN/EAN: 9783337164126

Printed in Europe, USA, Canada, Australia, Japan

Cover: Foto ©Thomas Meinert / pixelio.de

More available books at **www.hansebooks.com**

BRITISH MUSEUM.

GUIDE

TO

THE EXHIBITION

OF

CHINESE AND JAPANESE PAINTINGS

IN THE

PRINT AND DRAWING GALLERY.

PRINTED BY ORDER OF THE TRUSTEES.

1888.

PRICE TWOPENCE.

THE building containing the galleries in which are exhibited the Museum Glass and Ceramic collections, and, at present, Chinese and Japanese Drawings selected from the series purchased from Mr. William Anderson, has been erected from funds bequeathed by Mr. William White, who died on the 13th of May, 1823. By his will, dated the 10th of December, 1822, he directed that, on the death of his wife and child, his landed property, consisting of an estate named Hildern and Holms, near Botley, in Hampshire, and houses in Cowes, Isle of Wight, and, after payment of legacies, his personal estate, on the death of his wife, should revert to the Trustees of the British Museum. The claim of the Trustees to the landed property was disputed, and by a decree in the Vice-Chancellor's court, July 1826, disallowed, the devise to the Museum being pronounced to be invalid as within the provisions of the statute of mortmain. Upon the death of the widow in the year 1879, the Trustees became entitled under the will to a sum of £63,941 in various Government stocks, realizing with dividends the amount of £71,780, reduced however to £65,411 by payment of legacy duty exacted by the Treasury.

The strong interest in the Museum shown by this disposal of his property by Mr. White, was probably in a great measure excited by his having been brought up in its near neighbourhood; his father having lived in Soho Square, and he himself in Store Street and in Tavistock Square. The Museum collections as he knew them were closely packed in Montagu House, their original repository; the only addition to which, at the date of the will, were rooms on the west side built for reception of the Elgin and the Townley marbles. The Library was increasing, and had received large accessions by bequests from the Rev. C. M. Cracherode and Sir Joseph Banks, as well as from other donations. It was

also already known that the splendid library formed by
George the Third was to be made over to the nation, and
the difficulty of housing it must have been under discussion.
Undoubtedly the straitened condition of the Museum collections, no less than the importance of the institution
itself, was in Mr. White's mind when he decided on his
bequest ; and this shows itself in the terms of the will
directing its application.   He does not make it an imperative
condition that the money should be expended on an enlarge-
ment of the building, but he suggests it very decidedly.   His
words are :—" The money and property so bequeathed to the
British Museum I wish to be employed in building or im-
proving upon the said institution, and that round the frieze of
some part of such building, or, if this money is otherwise
employed, then over or upon that which so employed it, the
words Gulielmus White, Arm. Britt. dicavit 18—, be carved,
or words to that import "—adding, apologetically, in reference
to the ostentation betrayed in this instruction, " It is a little
vanity of no harm, and may tempt others to follow my example
in thinking more of the nation and less of themselves."

What appears to have been his wish has happily been
carried out by the application of the bequest exclusively to
building purposes.   In respect to the patriotic sentiment in
the latter part of the quotation from the will, the reflection may
arise that Mr. White may have been sacrificing the interests
of his son to a generous consideration for his country.   A
further extract, containing the clause of the bequest, shows
how he deliberately regarded his son's interest : "If my widow
shall marry again, or after her decease, my executors shall
immediately then transfer and pay over the residue of my
property   .   .   .   unto the governors for the time being of
that national institution, the British Museum.   .   .   .   For
from the nation my property came, and when I leave my son
enough to be a farmer, he has that which may make him as
happy and respectable as he can be in any station, and it is
my charge that he be so brought up."   He in fact left his
landed property for this purpose ; but the son died in his
infancy.

Mrs. White outlived her husband for a period of fifty-six

years, and it was not till the year 1879 that the Trustees of the Museum took the benefit of the bequest. It came to them very opportunely, for at that time Government was spending large sums on a new building for the Natural History departments, and was altogether inaccessible to appeals for similar outlay at Bloomsbury, where, notwithstanding the great gain of space obtained by the separation of these collections, there was still urgent need of further accommodation for some of the departments. The Greek and Roman sculptures wanted space for proper arrangement; relief was urgently demanded for the crowded state of the Reading Room; the department of Manuscripts was destitute of a suitable room for readers consulting the select MSS. used only under special supervision; and the department of Prints and Drawings had been waiting many years for space adapted to the growth of the collections and for their exhibition. All these wants were very pressing, and they were met more or less satisfactorily by the help of Mr. White's bequest. A gallery was built in connection with the department of Greek and Roman antiquities for the better display of the remains of the Mausoleum of Halicarnassos; and an extensive building was erected on the south-eastern side of the Museum, with front to Montagu Street, and with wings on each side connecting it with the main building. Within this new structure a Reading Room for newspapers has been opened, and space found for storage of the London journals and parliamentary papers. Working rooms have been provided for the department of Manuscripts, and additional space for its collections. The Ceramic and Glass collections have gained a well-lighted gallery; and the entire department of Prints and Drawings has obtained convenient accommodation, with a large gallery for the exhibition of its treasures.

Of the personal history of Mr. White there is little to be said, for he was cut off very early in life. His family was connected with Haseley Court and Newington in Oxfordshire. His father was John White, son of George, for some years Clerk to the Committees of Privileges and Elections of the House of Commons; and his mother was Catharine Leigh, of the Isle of Wight. He was born in the year 1800; and, having entered the University of Oxford as a Commoner of Brasenose College, took his degree in 1820, and was subsequently called to the Bar. He married Caroline Avis Bull, daughter of John Bull, Esq., Surgeon, of Oxford, and had one son, who died in infancy. Mr. White died in the year 1823. The portrait prefixed to this notice is copied from a miniature in the possession of his brother-in-law, the Rev. Henry Bull, Honorary Canon of Christchurch, Oxford, and Rector of Lathbury, in Buckinghamshire. This gentleman, now in his ninety-first year, and probably the only person who retains a personal recollection of Mr. White, describes him as having been highly intelligent, with scientific tastes, and fond of art.

EDWARD A. BOND.

February, 1888.

PREFACE.

THE present Exhibition consists of a selection from the extensive collection of Japanese and Chinese paintings purchased for the Museum in 1881 from Mr. William Anderson, F.R.C.S., formerly medical officer to Her Majesty's Legation, Japan. That collection has been fully described in the official catalogue prepared by Mr. Anderson, and published by order of the Trustees in 1886. The subject has been further treated by the same author in his illustrated work, *The Pictorial Arts of Japan*, published in the same year. To these books, as well as to the work of M. Gonse, *L'Art Japonais*, the student is referred for more detailed information than the limits of the present guide admit concerning the history of the several schools and masters represented, and the nature and meaning of the subjects which they depict.

Great as has been the interest and admiration long felt in Europe and America for the minor and industrial arts of the Japanese, the history and productions of their regular schools of painting had attracted comparatively little attention previously to the researches made by Mr. Anderson during his residence in the country. Other inquirers have since taken up the study, and other collections have been formed, notably that of Professor Fenollosa in America, and those of M. Bing and M. Gonse in Paris, and of Messrs. Dillon, Phené Spiers and Ernest Hart in England. Hence, and by the help of the detailed biographical and critical treatises in the native literature, and of the traditions preserved by native experts, it has become possible to establish trustworthy principles and tests for the historical and technical classification of the class of works in question. At the same time the practice, which has prevailed for centuries, of copying and repeating the original works of distinguished masters, and the frequent addition to pictures of false seals and signatures, render much caution necessary in individual cases of attribution, especially among the works of the oldest schools and painters. In the preparation of his volumes above quoted, Mr. Anderson used every available means of investigation, and has accepted no attribution that has not the authority of the most accredited native experts. The present guide is in the main simply a compilation and abridgment from his work, with a few additions and corrections derived partly from the author himself and partly from other sources. To Mr. Henry Seebohm and Mr. James Britten I am particularly indebted for help in identifying the birds and the plants respectively which are figured in the drawings of natural history.

In studying the pictorial art of the Japanese, with that of the early Chinese masters from which it was derived, it is essential to bear in mind the character of their artistic ideals and traditions, which in some respects differ radically from our own. To reproduce on the painted surface, in the Western manner, all the parts of any given scene of nature, in the actual truth of their appearand relations, is not the task they have proposed to themselves ; and of the scientific aids requisite to such an attempt they have accordingly remained contentedly ignorant,—of linear perspective almost entirely (while handling aerial perspective with great, though generally quite arbitrary, skill),—of the anatomical structure of men and animals hardly less. They do not try to express relief and solidity by means of natural light and shade, and they indicate the phenomena of day and night, not by difference of illumination, but merely by the introduction of a conventional red disk for the sun, and a white disk or crescent for the moon. Their art is thus essentially one of decoration, convention, and suggestion. Beauty and vivacity of decorative effect : in regard to touch and handling, the utmost attainable degree at once of decision and sensitiveness : and in regard to nature, a system of extreme simplification and abstraction, combined with the most expressive and direct rendering of the vital facts of form, movement and character, in the elements selected : these, speaking generally, are the qualities at which they aim, and which they often achieve— especially in designs taken from the life of animals and plants—with a perfection to which the art of the West hardly affords a parallel.

Chinese and Japanese paintings are executed generally on silk, sometimes on paper. The material employed is exclusively water-colour, sometimes pure and sometimes opaque, and the tools brushes of various sorts and sizes.

The technical terms used in the following pages are these :—

Kakémono = hanging picture, which when complete is always fitted with a border of coloured silks, arranged according to certain prescribed schemes, and with a roller at the lower end by which it is rolled up when not suspended for exhibition. The silk border is regarded as forming decoratively an essential part of every picture. As it wears out it is from time to time renewed, so that comparatively few works of the very early masters are found retaining their original borders.

Makimono = roll, that is a picture painted, so to speak, panorami-cally, along a number of continuous strips of paper or silk fastened together. Such rolls are often many yards in length, and seldom more than twelve or fifteen inches in depth. They are furnished with a roller at one end, and only un-rolled when required for inspection.

Gaku = a picture stretched and framed in a wooden (generally lacquered) frame.

The following are the authorities referred to :—

A., *Cat.* = Anderson, William, *Descriptive and Historical Catalogue of a Collection of Japanese and Chinese Paintings in the British Museum.* Printed by order of the Trustees. London (Long-mans, Quaritch, Trübner), 1886.

A., *P. A. J.* = Anderson, William, *The Pictorial Arts of Japan.* London : Sampson Low, 1886.

The Exhibition is arranged in two series. The first series, com-prising nos. 1–133, and consisting mainly of kakémonos, besides a few makimonos, gakus, and screen pictures, is shown (with the exception of the two screen pictures, 61* and 69) in the cases round the walls of the room. The second series, comprising nos. 134–173, and consisting of drawings either unmounted or newly mounted in the European manner (but on Japanese paper) is placed in the cases standing on the floor.

SIDNEY COLVIN.

PLAN OF GALLERY.

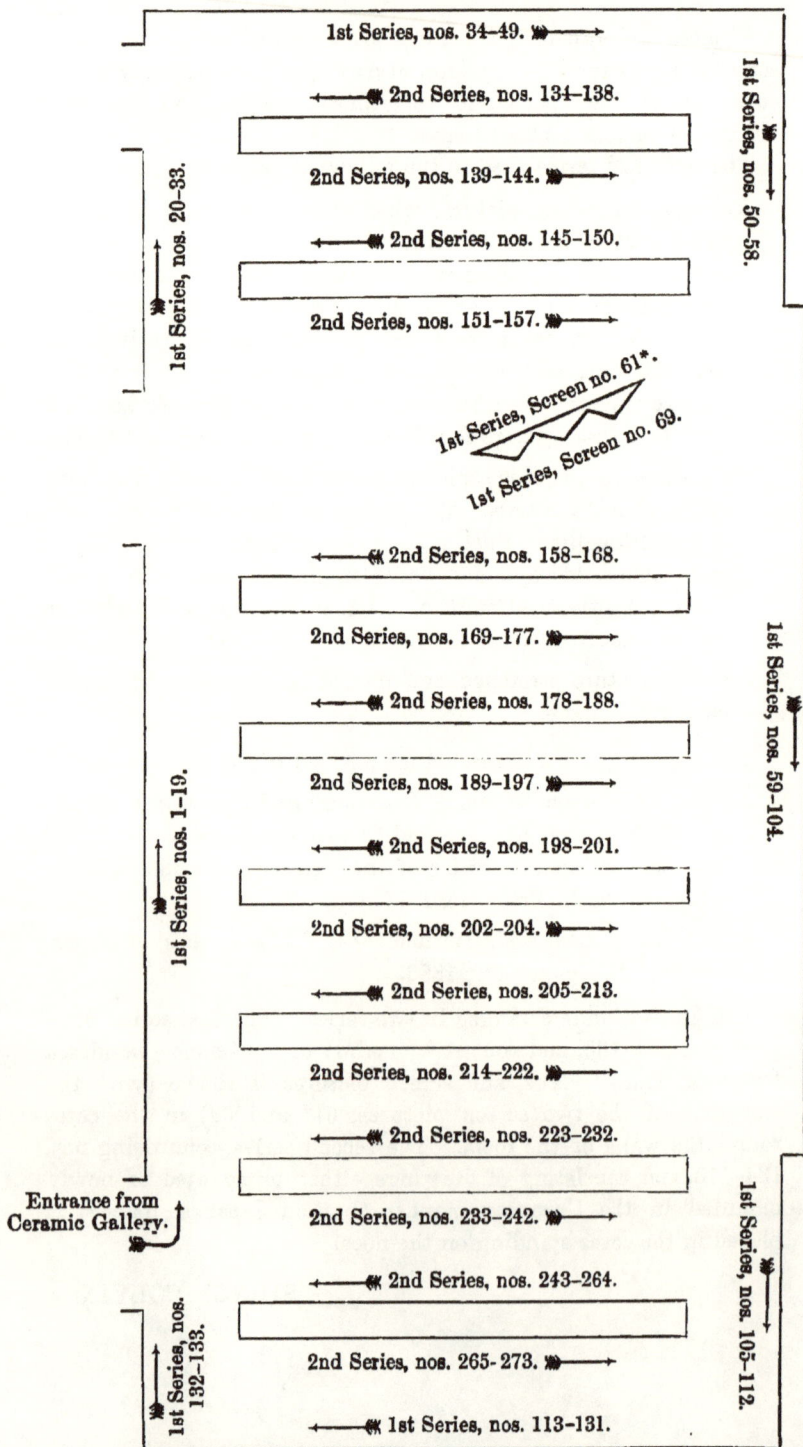

1st Series, nos. 34–49. ⟫⟶

⟵⟪ 2nd Series, nos. 134–138.

2nd Series, nos. 139–144. ⟫⟶

⟵⟪ 2nd Series, nos. 145–150.

2nd Series, nos. 151–157. ⟫⟶

1st Series, Screen no. 61*.

1st Series, Screen no. 69.

⟵⟪ 2nd Series, nos. 158–168.

2nd Series, nos. 169–177. ⟫⟶

⟵⟪ 2nd Series, nos. 178–188.

2nd Series, nos. 189–197. ⟫⟶

⟵⟪ 2nd Series, nos. 198–201.

2nd Series, nos. 202–204. ⟫⟶

⟵⟪ 2nd Series, nos. 205–213.

2nd Series, nos. 214–222. ⟫⟶

⟵⟪ 2nd Series, nos. 223–232.

2nd Series, nos. 233–242. ⟫⟶

⟵⟪ 2nd Series, nos. 243–264.

2nd Series, nos. 265–273. ⟫⟶

⟵⟪ 1st Series, nos. 113–131.

1st Series, nos. 20–33.

1st Series, nos. 1–19.

Entrance from Ceramic Gallery. ⟶

1st Series, nos. 132–133.

1st Series, nos. 50–58.

1st Series, nos. 59–104.

1st Series, nos. 105–112.

FIRST SERIES.

The numbers of this series follow along the walls from left to right, beginning at the entrance from the Ceramic Gallery (see plan).

CHINESE PAINTINGS (nos. 1-10).

The pictorial arts of Japan being essentially derivative from those of China, the first place in the Exhibition has been given to specimens of early Chinese painting of the Sung, Yüen,. and Ming dynasties (10th–16th centuries). Such works are not only excessively rare in themselves, but have at all times been valued above all others by the artists and connoisseurs of Japan.

The paintings of the early Chinese school are as to subject of two main kinds, sacred and secular. The sacred or Buddhistic division includes (*a*) representations of the subordinate personages of the Buddhist religion—saints and supernatural beings—freely exhibited, singly or in groups, in the ordinary guise of humanity, with natural surroundings and attributes : and (*b*) elaborate conventional or hieratic compositions illustrating the mysteries of the faith according to prescribed schemes, in which the whole arrangement and every detail are charged with symbolic and ritual meaning. The secular division includes portraits of famous personages, and representations of landscape and natural history. The latter class of subjects are often treated in monochrome, often slightly touched with colour, and sometimes fully coloured, but in every case freely and rapidly sketched in a liquid medium and with a full brush, the subject chosen being simplified by the selection of its most vital and striking elements and the exclusion of all embarrassing details. The elements so selected are expressed, in the works of the early Chinese masters, in a manner in which dignity of style is singularly combined with rapidity and sweep of hand : it having been above all things required of the painter that his work should exhibit the same freedom and certainty of touch as was displayed by the masters of calligraphic handwriting,—an art which among these races both demanded far more skill, and earned far higher rewards and reputation, than in the West.

The early history of Chinese pictorial art is very obscure. Native authors allude to it as one of ' the six branches of calli-

graphy'—that which teaches 'the forms of matter'—and thus
refer its origin to the legendary era; but no satisfactory record of
the name and achievements of any individual painter appears
before the third century A.D., nearly two hundred years after the
importation from India of the Buddhistic pictures and images.
It was this importation which probably gave the start in China to
a new and more ambitious phase of a previously undeveloped art.

The first painter whose name has been found in history was
TSAO FUH-HING, who served under the Emperor Sun Küan in the
third century A.D. He was noted for the delineation of figures
and dragons, and is said to have executed Buddhist pictures for
the temples which were then becoming rapidly multiplied.

The next artist, concerning whom any precise information is
attainable, was CHANG SANGYIU, who lived about the middle of
the sixth century, and was engaged by the devout monarch,
WU TI, as a painter of Buddhist pictures. It is uncertain
whether any of his works are now in existence, but his name
is frequently referred to as that of a master whose style was
imitated by many later celebrities.

The principal artists of the seventh century were YEN LITEH;
his younger brother, YEN LIPUN, who is chiefly remembered by
a series of portrait studies of historical paragons of learning and
loyalty; and CHANG YÜEH, who lived a little later than these,
and though greatly esteemed as a painter, is better known as the
Minister of State to the Emperor HÜAN TSUNG. He died A.D. 730,
at the age of sixty-three.

Several famous painters left their mark on the history of the
eighth century. The greatest of these was WU TAO-TSZ', who
was engaged as a court artist by the Emperor MING HWANG.
It was only after a long struggle against poverty, and a failure to
succeed as a calligraphist, that he turned his attention to painting.
In style, he followed the masterpieces of CHANG SANGYIU, with
whom he was declared to be identified by metempsychosis. He
became especially famous as a designer of Buddhist pictures, and
his portraitures of Kwanyin and certain other divinities are still
regarded as the models for priestly artists; his landscapes were of
extraordinary vigour, and full of picturesque beauty; and his
delineations of animals are said to have been life-like to an illusive
degree.

His works are now chiefly known by copies, some of which are
marked by a force and unconventionality rarely seen in the
paintings of later artists; but the specimens are insufficient to
allow a fair judgment of his capabilities. An original altar-piece,
representing the *Nirvāna* of Sākyamuni, is preserved at the temple
of Manjuji, in Kioto, and by dignity of composition, and the extraordinary truth of expression and action marking the figures of the
weeping divinities and disciples, manifests a genius possessed by
few of the Buddhistic artists of later centuries, who have indeed
been content to copy the design of this great master of the Tang

dynasty with a fidelity that speaks volumes as to their estimation of the original.

The names of famous Chinese artists of the Sung dynasty (A.D. 960–1206) have reached us in numbers too considerable to be quoted: but works by or attributed to several of the chief among them, as HWEI TSUNG, MA YÜEN, MUH KI, MI FUH, and NGAN HWUI, will be found in the first section of the Exhibition. Still more numerous are the lists of painters belonging to the succeeding Yüen and Ming dynasties.

During the first half of the period covered by the latter dynasty the art retained much of its earlier style and excellence; but during the second half (about 1450–1628) a decadence set in, partly owing to the spread of a facile and mannered way of work which had its origin in Southern China, and gradually infected the more virile style of the North. That decadence has never since been arrested; and during the last three-and-a-half centuries the Japanese schools of painting have been far more distinguished for energy and fertility, power of invention and skill of hand, than the school of China, from whose example, in earlier ages, they had once and again drawn all the best of their inspiration.

1. White Eagle on Perch.
Attributed to the Emperor HWEI TSUNG: Sung dynasty, reigned A.D. 1101–1126.

Kakémono on silk, in colours (A., *Cat.* p. 495, no. 2).

This Emperor was famous for drawings of falcons.

2. Wild Geese in the Rushes.
Painted by HWUI SU: Sung dynasty, twelfth century.

Kakémono on silk, in monochrome (A., *Cat.* p. 495, no. 3).

The bird represented is the Chinese goose (*Anser cygnoides*).

3. Eagle on Oak-bough.
Attributed to MUH KI: Sung dynasty, twelfth century.

Kakémono on silk, in monochrome (A., *Cat.* p. 497, no. 9).

The bird represented is the Crested Hawk-Eagle (*Spiraetus nipaulensis*).

4. Cock and Chicken, with a Peony.
Painted by WANG TS'UEN: Sung dynasty, twelfth century.

Kakémono on silk, in colours (A., *Cat.* p. 495, no. 4).

5. Three Rishis in the Wilderness.
Painted by NGAN HWUI: Sung and Yüen dynasties, thirteenth century.

Kakémono on silk, in colours (A., *Cat.* p. 496, no. 6).

The Rishis (Ch. Sien Nung; Jap. Sennin) are creations of philosophy and superstition, who play a great part in the mythology, compounded of Taoist and Buddhist elements, of China and Japan. They are variously classified, but the grouping which accords best with references in Sinico-Japanese literature is that given by Eitel in his ' Handbook of Chinese Buddhism ' :—1. Deva Ṛishis, who are believed to reside in the Seven Circular Rocks which surround Mount Meru.—2. Spirit Ṛishis, who roam about in the air. —3. Human Ṛishis, or recluses who have obtained the charm of immortality.—4. Earth Ṛishis, who live in subterranean caves.—5. Preta Ṛishis, who either roam about unseen, or live on islands, in deserts, or in caverns.—Of these five classes the third is the most familiar to students of Chinese and Japanese religious and legendary art. Among the many figures of this class whose portraitures occur in paintings and books, most can be recognised by their attributes, and the stories concerning them are stories (generally very vague) of mortals who by solitude, discipline, and the use of elixirs, have acquired supernatural powers and exemption from death. The three personages here shown, seated round a bronze vessel placed on a rock, are respectively identified as CHUNGLI KÜAN (Jap. SHŌRIKEN), LÜ TUNG PIN (Jap. RIŌTOHIN), and LI T'IEH K'WAI (Jap. RI TEKKAI). The pine and wild plum in the landscape are emblems of longevity.

6. A Crane Settling (*Grus viridirostris*).
Painted by MI FUH : Sung dynasty, 1051-1107.

Kakémono on silk, in colours (A., *Cat.* p. 498, no. 15 ; where, however, the painter is wrongly named. The signature is that of MI FUH, otherwise known as MI YÜEN CHANG : see A., *Cat.* p. 487).

One of a pair : the companion piece, also representing a crane of the same species (the sacred or Manchurian crane) is not exhibited.

7. A Sage and his Attendant in the Wilderness.
Painted by CHÊN CHUNG-FUH : Ming dynasty, fifteenth century.

Kakémono on silk, in colours (A., *Cat.* p. 497, no. 13).

The personages represented are not identified. The picture is accompanied by a eulogium of the painter, who is said to have drawn the portrait of the Emperor.

8. Wild Geese in the Rushes (*Anser segetum*).
Painted by LIN LIANG : Ming dynasty, sixteenth century.

Kakémono on silk, in monochrome (A., *Cat.* p. 499, no. 27).

One of a pair : the companion piece, also representing geese and water-plants, is not exhibited.

9. Magpies, Bamboos, and Peach.
Painted by Lü Kɪ : Ming dynasty, sixteenth century.

Kakémono on silk, the peach-blossoms coloured, the rest in monochrome (A., *Cat.* p. 500, no. 34).

10. Philosopher and Disciples.
Painted by Sɪ-kɪɴ Kü-tszE : Ming dynasty, fifteenth century.

Kakémono on paper, in colours (A., *Cat.* p. 500, no. 37).

The personage represented has not been identified. He is shown seated in a large chair and holding a palm-leaf fan. On the right is a boy carrying a tray on which are some lacquered cups with golden spoons; towards the left stand two men, probably disciples, and against these a boy with a case of books. A very small white horse is tied to a lacquered post in the foreground near the middle of the picture. The principal accessories are a tortoise, a stag, a crane, and a pine-tree, all emblematic of longevity. A large screen appears behind the philosopher's seat. The types, costumes, and details are distinctively Korean rather than Chinese. The drawing of the heads is marked by extraordinary individuality and precision, while the figures are unfinished, the feet ill drawn, and the animals treated conventionally. In the native certificate the subject is described as a ' Chinese Emperor,' but this is evidently an error.

PAINTINGS PROBABLY CHINESE (nos. 11–13).

The following three Buddhistic pictures were sold in Japan as examples of Japanese art, the pair nos. 11 and 12 being attributed to Chō Densu (see below no. 14), and no. 13 to a pupil of Sesshiū (see below nos. 59, 60, 61). But these attributions are contested by some of the best experts on technical grounds, and it seems certain that they are all three in; reality original works of Chinese painting; nos. 11 and 12 especially works of a very high antiquity.

11. An Arhat and an Apsaras.
Painter unknown : Sung dynasty, eleventh century ?

Kakémono on silk, in colours ; much darkened by age (A., *Cat.* p. 66, no. 1).

The Arhats (Jap. Rakan) are the primitive disciples and apostles of the Buddhist faith, and are always represented in priestly and saintly aspect. The individual here depicted cannot be identified. He wears rings in his elongated ear-lobes, and holds a Buddhist *Nio-i*: the Apsaras kneeling before him holds an offering of peaches and a flowering branch of the peach-tree of Longevity. The picture is one of a pair : see next number.

12.   **The Arhat Bhadra.**
      Painter unknown : Sung dynasty, eleventh century?
      Companion piece to the above (A., *Cat.* p. 66, no. 2).

The emblematical tiger sufficiently distinguishes the Arhat
Bhadra : who is moreover conspicuous by his elongated
eye-brows and ear-lobes.

13.   **Vimalakirti.**
      Painter unknown : Ming dynasty, fifteenth century?
      Kakémono on silk, in colours (A., p. 270, no. 1207, *P. A. J.* pl. 18).

Vimalakīrti was a famous Indian priest, said to have been a
contemporary of Ṣākyamuni, and to have visited China.
He is portrayed in priestly garb, seated on a mat, and
holding a *futsujin* or clerical brush : his head surrounded
by a colourless nimbus, the mark of the Arhat.   The work
shows great individuality of character, and power both of
design and handling.

JAPANESE PAINTINGS.

The knowledge of the art of painting was unquestionably
imported into Japan from China; both directly, it would seem,
and indirectly through the painters of Korea.

The written documents of the eighth and ninth centures, which
comprise the oldest known records of the Japanese, make no
allusion to the existence of any phase of pictoral art before the
fifth century A.D.   The first painter they mention was a Chinese
immigrant of royal descent, known by the names of NANRIŪ and
SHINKI.   This artist is said to have come to Japan during the
reign of the Emperor YŪRIAKU (457–479 A.D.), and was hospitably
received by the ruling powers.   He ended his days in his adopted
country, leaving descendants who for many generations held
honourable positions in the Imperial service.   The fifth in succes-
sion from NANRIŪ is especially noticed as having received from
the Mikado the title of *Yamato Yéshi* (painter of Japan), and from
the Empress SHŌTOKU, in 770 A.D., the name of ŌŌKA NO IMIKI.
The existence of this family may doubtless be admitted as a fact,
but we know nothing as to the nature of their artistic achievements.

It is probable, however, that Japanese art education made little
progress until the introduction of Buddhism in the middle of the
sixth century, when the early native workers, guided by Korean
instructors, first tried their hands upon Buddhistic pictures and
images, beginning, at the same time, to acquire a knowledge of
the more graphic Korean and Chinese styles of painting, as well as
of many other branches of art.

The first and somewhat nebulous period of the history of
Japanese painting is brought to a close in the latter half of the ninth

century, when a fresh impulse was given to the art by the works
and example of one of the greatest painters to which the country
has given birth. Kosé no Kanaoka rose into fame in the time of
the Emperor Seiwa (850–859). Born in the midst of an accom-
plished court, he lacked neither opportunity nor encouragement.
He had access to the works of the best periods of Chinese and
Korean art, executed before the dilettanteism of the Southern
School had created a false ideal, and is said to have selected, as the
model upon which his style was founded, the pictures of Wu T'ao-
tsz', the greatest painter of the T'ang dynasty. The extraordinary
reputation which Kanaoka acquired during his lifetime, and
handed down to posterity, is of a kind that leaves no doubt as to
the reality of his talents. The references to his works are precise,
and date from the period of their production. As might be sur-
mised, however, few of them have survived the lapse of ten centuries; hence the range of his powers must be accepted to a great
extent upon tradition. He is said to have excelled in landscapes,
figures, and horses; but unfortunately no examples of his skill
in these directions have been preserved. All that remain to
represent his genius are a few Buddhistic paintings, but some
of these attest sufficiently his admirable powers of design and
colouring. The pictures most frequently referred to in the records
of his time were portraits of Chinese sages, painted by command
of the Emperors under whom he served, and of these works several
were preserved for many centuries until they fell a sacrifice to fire,
the great enemy of all the relics of antiquity in Japan.

The interval between the appearance of Kanaoka and the
fifteenth century constitutes what may be defined as the second
period in the history of Japanese art. The Kosé line, or descendants of the great Kanaoka, may be traced throughout this period,
and were in repute chiefly as painters of Buddhist ritual pictures.
Side by side with them other artists continued to carry on, with
more or less of fidelity, the traditions of the Chinese school; while
during the eleventh century a new and native manner of painting
was evolved, marked by several peculiar characteristics of its own,
and known as the *Yamato-Riū.* Its reputed founder was a pupil of
the Kosé line named Kasuga Motomitsu; its head in the thirteenth century one Fujiwara no Tsunétaka, who assumed the
family name of Tosa; and this name was thenceforth adopted by
his followers and descendants as the permanent title of the
academy.

These three schools, or more properly styles (for a single master
might work according to each in turn)—the Buddhist, the Yamato-
Tosa, and the Chinese—continued to prevail exclusively in Japanese
painting during what we have called its second period; that
is from the ninth until the beginning of the fifteenth century,
when a great and general Renaissance took place in the art. This
Renaissance consisted in the main of an enthusiastic return on
the part of the followers of the Chinese school to the examples of

the early masters of the T'ang, Sung, and Yüen dynasties, and had
for its consequence the foundation of several new academies by
masters avowedly basing their practice on those examples. But
the same period had also been marked by the appearance of the
greatest of all Japanese painters of Buddhist sacred personages—
MEICHŌ or CHŌ DENSU: and a striking reinvigoration of the power
of the Yamato-Tosa school soon followed in the hands of SHIBA
SONKAI, TOSA MITSUNOBU, and his son TOSA MITSUSHIGÉ.

Our exhibition of Japanese paintings contains no examples of
what have been above defined as the first and second periods of the
art; but opens with the period of Revival at the beginning of the
fifteenth century. The works exhibited are divided according to
the several schools or styles to which they belong, beginning with
the

BUDDHIST SCHOOL (nos. 14–19).

The production of Buddhist sacred representations had formed,
as has been indicated already, a large part of the practice of the
earliest Chinese, and following them of the earliest Japanese,
painters. There is no doubt that the first Buddhist painters of
China had been directly inspired by the specimens of Indian
Buddhist art imported into their country by the missionaries and
propagators of the faith between the first and sixth centuries A.D.
That this is so follows not only from antecedent historical pro-
bability, but from many direct evidences, such as the almost
invariable absence of Mongolian traits in the physiognomical
characters given by the Chinese to the various divinities of the
Buddhist pantheon, and the practical identity in point of dress,
attitude, and attributes, between Indian representations of certain
of the divine personages, and the corresponding images produced
in China and Japan. Again, in the colouring of Chinese Buddhistic
paintings, the selection and arrangement of pigment, while very
unlike the practice of the older secular school of China, often produce effects that strongly recall those of Indian work. On the
other hand, many of the Western types were modified in the
course of their adoption into the Middle Kingdom, not only by the in-
fusion of new elements of artistic style, but more particularly by the
incorporation of a symbolism appertaining to pre-existing beliefs
in the latter country.

The *Butsu-yé*, as the Japanese call the religious picture of the
true Buddhist school or style, has certain distinctive peculiarities
that separate it from the works of all the secular schools and styles.

While the chief ideal of the older Chinese painters, and of their
Japanese imitators, in secular art, was calligraphic dexterity, the
Buddhist artist—at least in temple pictures of the hieratic or
ritual class (see above, p. 7)—aimed principally at gorgeousness
and impressiveness of effect. The Sketch was replaced by the
Illumination. The first, with its sober monochrome or subdued
local tints, and its bold sweeping stroke of pencil, appealed chiefly

to the educated perceptions of the few : while the other aimed at
attracting the untrained senses of the people by a gorgeous but
studied play of gold and colour, and a richness of mounting and
accessories, that appear strangely at variance with the begging
bowl and patched garments of primitive Buddhism.

Gold was the one thing essential to the Buddhist altar-piece,
and sometimes when applied upon a black ground is the only
material used.   In all cases it is employed with an unsparing
hand.   It appears in uniform masses, as in the body of the Buddha
or in the golden lakes of the Western paradise; in minute diapers
upon brocades and clothing; in circlets or undulating rays, to form
the glory surrounding the head of Amitābha; in raised bosses and
rings upon the armlets or necklets of the Bodhisattvas and Devas,
and in a hundred other manners.   The pigments chosen to har-
monise with this display are necessarily body-colours of the most
pronounced hues, untoned by any trace of chiaroscuro.   Such
materials as these would sorely try the average artist, but the
Oriental painter knows how to dispose them without risk of
crudity or gaudiness, and the precious metal, however lavishly
applied, is generally distributed over the picture with a judgment
that would make it difficult to alter or remove any part without
detriment to the beauty of the work.

Drawing in Buddhist art held a place to some extent secondary
to that of the colouring.   It varied considerably in style, was
sometimes stiff and formal, at others free and graceful, and in the
pictures of Chō Densu and the older Yamato artists often assumed
the vigorously graphic type characteristic of the great T'ang
masters.

Of invention little can be said.   Workers in this style have from
first to last been fettered by traditions considered almost holy in
their antiquity and origin, and many remarkable painters down to
the present century have exhausted their faculties in mere repetition of hieratic types and compositions handed down to them ages
before by Koreans and Chinese, feeling most proud when their
labour was thought a worthy copy of a foreign original.

14. An Arhat with a Lion.
Painted by Chō Densu : 1351–1427.

Kakémono on silk, in colours (A., *Cat.* p. 66, no. 3, *P. A. J.* pl. 8).

Meichō, better known as Chō Densu, a priest of the temple of
Tōfukuji, in Kioto, was an older contemporary of the
Italian painter-monk Fra Angelico, and offers a curious
parallel to his European brother in talent, character, and
calling.   His skill is the subject of fabulous legends, and
many anecdotes record the unsought fame won by the
simple mind, devout belief, and indifference to temporal
rewards, that maintained him throughout the long years of

his life in the seclusion of the monastic retreat which
derives its chief renown from the fruits of his labours. He
died in 1427, at the age of seventy-six. The personage
here depicted cannot be certainly identified.

15. The Thirteen Buddhas.
Painter unknown : fifteenth century?

Kakémono on silk, in colours (A., *Cat.* p. 72, no. 25).

The figures depicted are arranged as follows:—

	Akāsagarbha.	
Amitābha.	Akshobhya.	Vairochhana.
Mahāsthāmaprāpta.	Avalokiteṣvara.	Bhaishajya Guru.
Maitreya.	Kshitigarbha.	Samantabhadra.
Mañjuṣrī.	Ṣākyamuni.	Achalā.

This picture offers an admirable example of the firm delicacy
of outline and harmony of colouring of the earlier *Butsu-yé,*
or Buddhist temple-pictures of Japan.

16. Amitābha and Bodhisattvas.
Painter unknown : eighteenth century.

Kakémono on silk, in colours (A., *Cat.* p. 74, no. 29).

Amitābha (Jap. Amida), the most popular Buddha both in
China and Japan, is one of the inventions of the Mahāyāna
school, and dates from about 300 A.D. He is supposed to
preside with Kwanyin (Avalokiteṣvara) over the Paradise in
the West, where the good may enjoy long ages of rest, but
without interruption to the circle of transmigrations. He
here appears surrounded by his retinue of the ' Twenty-five
Bodhisattvas,' most of whom have feminine forms, and are
playing upon instruments of music. The space around the
heavenly choir is filled with floating lotus-petals, flowers,
and divine images.

17. Amitābha.
Painted by Zō-jō-ji Dai-Sō-jō (chief priest of the temple of
Zōjōji): early nineteenth century.

Kakémono on silk, in colours (A., *Cat.* p. 67, no. 5, *P. A. J.* pl. 10).

Chinese Buddhists recognise nine forms of Amitābha, each
characterised by a peculiar position (*mudrā*) of the hands and
fingers. The form here represented is distinguished as
Jo-bon Jo-sho ('the first form, first birth'). The hands rest
upon the knees, palms upwards, and the fingers bent in such
a manner that the backs of the two last joints of the one hand
are in contact with the corresponding parts of the opposite
hand. The present is a peculiarly fine example of the
decorative and hieratic work of the Buddhist school in comparatively recent times.

18. The Amitābha Trinity.

Painted and written by EN-JIN-SAI : eighteenth century.

Kakémono on paper, in colours (A., *Cat.* p. 66, no. 4).

This picture has the peculiarity that the outlines of the three figures of Amitābha, Avalokiteṣvara, and Mahāsthāmaprāpta are formed by minutely written characters composing the Sūtras known in Japan as the *Sambu Kiō* and *Amida Kiō*. The first of these compositions is repeated thrice, the second twenty-five times.

19. Assemblage of Buddhist Divinities..

Painter unknown : seventeenth century.

Kakémono on silk, in colours (A., *Cat.* p. 81, no. 59).

The figures are too numerous for complete description. The principal image of the central group is that of Vâirôtchana (Dai Nichi Niorai). Above, below, to the left, and to the right of this are four Buddhas, viz., Akshobhya (East), Amitābha (West), Amogha (North), Ratnasambhava (South), and alternating with these are four Bodhisattvas. Beneath are three prominent figures, that in the middle line probably representing Akāṣagarbha, that on the left the Eleven-faced Kwanyin, that on the right another manifestation of Kwanyin. The remaining forms are mostly familiar groups of divinities, such as those of the Sixteen Bodhisattvas, the Twenty-five Bodhisattvas, the Seven Kwanyins, the Thirty-three Kwanyins, &c.

YAMATO-TOSA SCHOOL (nos. 20–33).

This is the oldest of the recognised native schools or styles of Japanese painting. Its foundation, as has been said, is attributed to KASUGA MOTOMITSU, who flourished in the beginning of the eleventh century, when it received the name of the *Yamato* or *Wagwa Riü:* and in the thirteenth century one of its chiefs, FUJIWARA NO TSUNÉTAKA, assumed the family name of TOSA, which has been adopted ever since by the members of the school as its permanent title. Of the various Japanese modifications of Chinese art, the works of the Yamato-Tosa School are in some senses the most characteristic, although those of its later periods (and the school has continued to subsist until the present century) are also the feeblest and most conventional. The drawings of the Yamato-Tosa artists are executed, as a rule, with finer pencils and a minuter finish than those of other schools, and, though sufficiently firm and delicate, look timid beside the Chinese art. But the beauty of the productions of this academy is most seriously marred by the incorrect and ungraceful rendering of the human figure, exemplified in the doll-like imbecility of their portraitures of the lords and ladies who represented the high culture of old

C

Kioto. This mannerism was perhaps rather the fault of a tradition than of any lack of artistic discrimination; for the same painters could, on occasion, abandon their formal and rather wearisome illustrations of Court life to dash off fresh and unconventional sketches, which displayed both the power of the Chinese School, and the humour of the modern artisan designers.

The colouring of the later *Yamato-yé* was as decorative as the use of gold and brilliant pigments could make it, and the coloured areas were so subdivided as to give almost the effect of a brocaded pattern; but although the disposition of contrasts was in some respects at variance with English canons, and a bright verdigris green was too freely used, the effect as a whole has much of the rich harmony of the illuminations of the fourteenth century missals.

One innovation in the practice of the Yamato artists was the expedient of spiriting away the roof from any building of which they desired to expose the interior. This licence appears to have no precedent in Chinese pictorial art.

The favourite motives of the school were drawn from biographies of famous scholars, priests, or heroes; poetical compositions; Chinese or native legends and romances—especially the *Genji Monogatari*, the *Sumiyoshi Monogatari*, the story of Urashima, the story of the Mugé-Hōjiu Gem, the Adventures of Raikō and his companions, and the history of the lives of Yoshitsuné and Benkei; temple inventories; and ceremonials of the Mikado's Court. The artists, however, frequently also painted Buddhist pictures, and moreover left many sketches of horses, birds, flowers, and other objects in the simple style of the old Chinese masters, as well as designs in a spirit of fun and caricature.

20. Horses at Exercise.
Attributed to To-sa Mitsu-nobu : fifteenth century.
Portion of a makimono, on paper, in colours (A., *Cat.* p. 155, no. 494, compare *P. A. J.*, fig. 121).

21, 22. Horses in their Stalls.
Attributed to To-sa Mitsu-shigé : sixteenth century.
Unmounted drawings, on paper, in colours (A., *Cat.* p. 150, nos. 422, 428).
From a set of twelve: the remainder of the set are not exhibited.

23. Quail and Millet.
Painter unknown : sixteenth century?
Kakémono on silk, in colours (A., *Cat.* p. 135, no. 256).
The quail in the Japanese picture is generally represented together with the millet, an association of ideas comparable with that which connects the swallow with the willow-tree, and the peacock with the peony. It is probable that nearly all of these groupings have their origin in famous poetical compositions.

24. Saigiō Hōshi at Kita Shirakawa.

Painted by To-sa Mitsu-nari : seventeenth century.

Kakémono on silk, in colours (A., *Cat.* p. 120, no. 204).

Satô Hioyé Norikiyo—better known as Saigiō Hōshi—was the seventh in descent from the famous Tawara Toda Hidésato, the slayer of the great Centipede. He held office in the Court of the Emperor Toba, but in the year 1137 abruptly abandoned his home and became a priest. Under the names of Eni and Saigiō he travelled through various parts of Japan, for self-discipline, until scarcely a place remained that he had not explored. He is celebrated as a poet, the most familiar of his compositions being a verse upon the Peerless Mountain. He died in 1198 at the age of seventy-three. He is here represented, as usual, in the dress of a travelling priest, with a staff and a very large hat, and stands in a listening attitude at the gate of a mansion. The perspective exposes the interior of a room, on the floor of which is seen a musical instrument (*biwa*). An inscription in grass characters appears at the upper part of the picture.

25. Robin and Waterfall.

Painted by Sumi-yoshi Hiro-michi : seventeenth century.

Kakémono on paper, in monochrome lightly touched with colour (A., *Cat.* p. 120, no. 202).

The bird represented is the Japanese Robin (*Erythræus akabigé*). The drawing is in a slight and sketchy manner less characteristic of the Tosa than of the earlier Chinese practice and that of the modern Japanese schools derivative from it.

26. The House of a Court Noble.

Said to be copied from a picture by Sumi-yoshi Hiro-chika : who worked in the fifteenth century.

Kakémono on silk, in colours (A., *Cat.* p. 124, no. 212).

The interior of the building is exposed by the curious artistic licence of removing the roof, a plan which is characteristic of this school, and which has also the advantage of displaying a greater amount of the scenery beyond. The dresses, the simplicity of furniture, the gorgeous decorative effects produced by screens and panels, are all deserving of notice, as illustrating the aspects of genuine ' high life ' in Japan.

27. Goshawk (*Astur palumbarius*) on perch.

Painted by Sumi-yoshi Hiro-masa (Ita-ya Kei-shiu): eighteenth century.

Kakémono on silk, in colours (A., *Cat.* p. 127, no. 228, *P. A. J.* pl. 61).

One of a pair : see next number. The vigorous and life-like drawing of these birds is curiously at variance with the laborious and conventional execution of the historical and semi-historical pictures by which the Tosa artists are best known. c 2

28. Goshawk on perch.
Painted by SUMIYOSHI HIROMASA (ITA-YA KEI-SHIU): eighteenth century.

Kakémono on silk, in colours (A., *Cat.* p. 127, no. 229).

Companion piece to the above.

29. The Seven Gods of Good Fortune.
Painted by SUMI-YOSHI HIRO-MASA (ITA-YA KEI-SHIU): eighteenth century.

Kakémono on silk, in colours (A., *Cat.* p. 127, no. 225).

The Seven Gods of Good Fortune (Jap. Shichifukujin), constituting a kind of popular appendage to the Buddhist pantheon, are the most familiar of all divinities in Japanese art, and though both their origin and functions are obscure, are at all times easily to be recognised by their attributes. In the present picture Fukurokujiu, the tall-headed, appears in the sky riding on a crane; while Bishamon, dressed as usual in armour, and retaining something of his Buddhistic dignity, stands next below. Beside him the female member of the group, Benten, plays on the *biwa*, and following in a semi-circle from right to left, Jurōjin wearing a high hat and fan, Hotei half disappearing in the huge bag on which he leans, Ébisu, having beside him in a basket the red *tai*-fish which is his emblem, and Daikoku reclining against his rice-bale and holding his mallet in his hand, all watch with upturned faces the approach of Fukurokujiu.

30. Scenes from the Genji Monogatari.
Painted by To-SA MITSU-YOSHI: eighteenth century.

Portion of a makimono, on paper, in colours (A., *Cat.* p. 137, no. 268).

The *Genji Monogatari*, one of the earliest of the Japanese romances, was written about the end of the tenth century by Murasaki Shikibu, a maid-of-honour to the lady who afterwards became the consort of the Emperor Ichijō. It consists of fifty-four chapters; the first forty-one relating to the life, adventures, and amorous intrigues of Prince Genji, a kind of Japanese Don Juan; the rest, (of which ten are supposed to have been added by the daughter of the authoress,) referring principally to the career of one of his sons. The period of time covered by the whole story is about sixty years, and the scenes are for the most part laid in Kioto.

31. Cranes (*Grus viridirostris*).
Painted by To-SA MITSU-SADA: 1805.

Kakémono on silk, in colours (A., *Cat.* 238).

32. Scenes from the Life of Hōnen Shōnin.

Painter unknown : sixteenth century?

Kakémono on silk (A., *Cat.* p. 134, no. 243).

One of a set of three : the other two are not exhibited.

The picture is subdivided by means of conventional clouds into a number of compartments, in which the different episodes of the story are represented, a device especially characteristic of this school. Hōnen Shōnin, known also as Enko Daishi, was born in 1133 in the province of Mimasaka, his birth being attended by various portents. At the age of fourteen he was sent to the great monastery of Hiyeizan, where he made rapid progress in study, and developed a special doctrine of salvation which became the creed of a new sect called the Jōdō-shiu. In 1207 he settled at Kiōto, and five years later died there at the age of seventy-nine.

33. The Night-March of the Hundred Demons.

Painted by SUMI-YOSHI HIRO-NAGA : nineteenth century.

Portion of a makimono, on paper, in colours (A., *Cat.* p. 136, no. 262).

A grotesque procession of demons, who are seen lightening the tedium of their journey by tricks and mockery, in travesty of the ceremonials of man, till we reach the van of the troop, who recoil and flee in confusion from the glare of the rising sun, which disperses the weird forms of the night-clouds. Copied from an ancient makimono by an unknown artist of the Tosa school, probably anterior to the fifteenth century.

[For other examples of the Yamato-Tosa School, see below, Second Series, nos. 134–157.]

CHINESE SCHOOL (nos. 34–58).

After the time of KANAOKA, through the greater part of the second period of Japanese painting, the authority of the early Chinese masters seems to have been comparatively weak, and their traditions to have languished, while the main strength of the artists of Japan was put forth in the production either of Buddhist temple-pictures, or of works in the Yamato-Tosa style last illustrated. But in the fifteenth century came a great and far-reaching revival of Chinese influence. The centre and starting-point of this influence was the school directed by JŌSETSU, a priest of Kiōto, in the first years of the fifteenth century.

After a profound study of the pictures of the celebrated artists of the Sung and Yüen dynasties, JŌSETSU established at the temple of Sōkokuji, in the Imperial city, a monastic academy for the promulgation of their teachings, and grouped around him a body of pupils destined to initiate a new departure in the art-history of their country. Little is known of this painter, and it is even

uncertain whether he was of Japanese or Chinese birth: his paintings, moreover, are too rare or questionable to furnish any safe
criterion of his powers. But by his teaching are said to have
been inspired the founders of three out of the four schools which
monopolised the attention of the artistic world in Japan down to
the middle of the last century; SHIŪBUN, SESSHIŪ, and KANO
MASANOBU.

To the two latter we shall come presently. The first, SHIŪBUN,
did not, as the others did, give his name to any new academy, but
must be regarded as the virtual founder of that which since his
time has been specifically known as the ' Chinese ' school of Japanese painting. To this school are reckoned as belonging all those
artists, down to the present century, who turning their backs
upon the native traditions of the courtly Yamato-Tosa style, have
practised according to Chinese example, without at the same time
enrolling themselves in any of the academies founded by and
named after particular masters who took part in the revival of the
Chinese taste.

Such artists, from the days of JŌSETSU almost to our own, have
been too numerous for any mention of even their leading names to
be attempted here. Several of them will be found characteristic-
ally represented in the following section of the Exhibition. Speaking generally, they have been accustomed to adopt not only the
style but the motives of the famous masters of the Sung and Yüen
dynasties, and to draw their historical, legendary, and religious
inspirations almost entirely from the literature or paintings of the
Middle Kingdom.

A vast number of their pictures are composed from no more
ambitious material than a slight reminiscence of vegetable life,
such as a limb of bamboo or pine, a peony or orchid, or a flowering
branch of plum or peach. Spirited and life-like sketches of birds,
of which the favourites were the crane, the hawk, the pheasant, the
peacock, the sparrow, the bunting, the quail, the starling, the fowl,
the cuckoo, and the wood-pigeon, were equally common, and in
most cases conveyed to the Chinese and Japanese a poetical or
emblematic meaning, that ensured a lasting popularity for the
motive. The examples selected from the mammalia were more
limited, being almost confined to the horse, the mule, the dog, the
ox, and a long-armed species of monkey. The tortoise and
serpent were the principal representatives of the reptiles; and
amongst fishes, the carp, as an emblem of perseverance, held the
highest place of honour. Insect life, except as an accessory, was
rather the property of a few individual painters than of the art.
Side by side with these creatures of the natural world, others
belonging to supernatural or mythical zoology — monstrous
animals and monstrous men of various significance and invention—
have abounded in the representations of this school.

The Chinese artist had a special predilection for the wilder
forms of picturesque beauty in landscape. Cascades, pools, and

streams; towering silicic peaks and rugged headlands; gnarled fantastic pines and plum-trees, side by side with the graceful stem and feathery foliage of the bamboo; mansions or pavilions crowning the heights or bordering the expanse of an inland lake, and straw-thatched cottages nestling in the valleys; these were elements that the Chinese landscape-painter lived to assort and reconstruct into a thousand pictures. The Japanese painters of the present and allied schools, seduced by the charms of this foreign ideal, were often led to neglect the more familiar attractions of their own scenery, and without having beheld any of the spots depicted by the old landscape masters of China, squandered an infinity of talent and ingenuity in building up new creations of their own with the material borrowed from their neighbours.

The most frequently repeated studies of the figure were calligraphic portraitures of Buddhist divinities, Taoist genii, and historical celebrities in the domains of war, politics or learning; with illustrations of historical events,—especially those belonging to the rise and fall of the Han dynasty (206 B.C.–220 A.D.),—and of tales of feudal devotion and of filial piety; designed commonly with much power, but showing little heed for academical truth. On the other hand, portraits from life, which were not rare, were almost always formal, ungraceful, and inexpressive, and stood at great disadvantage amongst the other pictorial works of the Chinese painter and of his Japanese imitator.

34. Chinese Landscape.
Painted by Shiū-bun: late fifteenth century.
Kakémono on paper, in monochrome (A., *Cat.* p. 197, no. 601, *P. A. J.* pl. 14).

This picture, attributed to the virtual founder of the school, is a typical example of its class. The scene is not studied from nature, but composed by a loving imitation of older Chinese models, and does not in any way represent the native landscape of Japan. The next five numbers all illustrate the same phase of art.

35. Chinese Landscape.
Painted by Riu-kiō: sixteenth century?
Fan-mount on paper, in monochrome, mounted as a kakémono (A., *Cat.* p. 108, no. 603).

36. Chinese Landscape.
Painted by Sō-ami : late fifteenth century.
Kakémono on paper, in monochrome (A., *Cat.* p. 198, no. 603).

37, 38. Chinese Landscapes; a pair.
Painted by Na-ra Hō-gen: fifteenth century.
Kakémonos on paper, in colours (A., *Cat.* p. 198, nos. 1135, 1136).

39. Chinese Landscape ; a panorama.
Painted by So-ga Ja-soku: fifteenth century.
Portion of a makimono, on paper, in monochrome (A., *Cat.* p. 248, no. 862, *P. A. J.* pl. 16).

40. Seiōbō and Mōjō Sennin.
Painted by YIU-HI : eighteenth century.

Kakémono on silk, in colours (A., *Cat.* p. 293, no. 778).

Seiōbō (Chinese Si Wang Mu),—a kind of Queen of the
Genii adopted by the Chinese Buddhists from the older
Taoist mythology, is identified by her tiara and the female
attendant carrying her fan; Mōjō (Chinese Mao Nū) by
her cloak of skins or leaves, and her emblem, the peach-
bloom of immortality. The deer at her side is also a symbol
of longevity.

41. Cat, Plants, and Insects.
Painter unknown : seventeenth century?

Kakémono on silk, in colours (A., *Cat.* p. 238, no. 804).

A masterpiece of somewhat indeterminate date and school.
The plants represented are amaranthus, convolvulus, and
two kinds of hibiscus.   The cat crouches, intently watching
an insect of the beetle tribe on a spray just over it, while
two other beetles are seen flying in the air above.

42. Chinese Scene: a Visit.
Painted by RIŪ-RI-KIŌ : eighteenth century.

Kakémono on silk, in colours (A., *Cat.* p. 200, no. 611).

One of a set of three : the two others are not exhibited.
Riūrikiō is specially noted for having introduced in Japan
imitations of a particular highly-coloured manner of painting
characteristic of the latest phase of Chinese art under the
Ming Dynasty.

43. Starlings on Bough (*Turdus cineraceus*): with Chrysan-
themum.
Painted by TŌ-SŌ: 1757.

Kakémono on silk, in colours (A., *Cat.* p. 231, no. 766).

44. The Fox Wedding.
Painted by KŌ-ZAN : nineteenth century.

Kakémono on silk, in colours (A., *Cat.* p. 214, no. 675).

Representations in which the ceremonies of mankind are
travestied by the lower animals are frequent in Japanese
art : compare below, no. 107.   The notion of the fox
wedding, however, belongs to the order of animal super-
stitions actually prevailing in rural Japan.

45. Squirrel and Vine : Moonlight.
Painted by SHI-KŌ SŌ-RIN : early nineteenth century.

Kakémono on silk, in monochrome (A., *Cat.* p. 228, no. 747).

46. Sparrows (*Passer montanus*) and Convolvulus.
Painted by SHI-KŌ SŌ-RIN : nineteenth century.

Kakémono on silk, in colours (A., *Cat.* p. 228, no. 778).

47. Buntings (*Emberiza rustica*) and Millet.
Painted by TAN-I BUN-CHŌ: early nineteenth century.

Kakémono on silk, in monochrome touched with colour (A., *Cat.* p. 243, no. 836).

48. Chinese Sage.
Painted by TAN-I BUN-CHŌ: 1797.

Kakémono on silk, in monochrome (A., *Cat.* p. 242, no. 829).

49. Carp.
Painted by TAN-I BUN-CHŌ: early nineteenth century.

Kakémono on silk, in colours (A., *Cat.* p. 243, no. 832).

50, 51. Flowers, a Pair.
Painted by TŌ-RIN: early nineteenth century.

Kakémono on silk, in colours (A., *Cat.* p. 230, nos. 760, 761).

The flowers represented in 50 are chrysanthemum, single peony, convolvulus, desmodeum, and a kind of everlasting: in 51, cherry, double peony, three kinds of iris, including the small *Iris japonica*, vetch, and Japanese violet.

52. Plum-blossom and full Moon.
Painted by UCHI-DA GEN-TAI: ninteenth century.

Kakémono on silk, in monochrome touched with colour (A., *Cat.* p. 205, no. 635).

53. Golden Pheasant (*Phasianus pictus*).
Painted by Ō-NISHI KEI-SAI: nineteenth century.

Kakémono on silk, in colours (A., *Cat.* p. 210, no. 661, *P. A. J.*, pl. 44).

54. Egrets (*Ardea modesta*) in Rain.
Painted by Ō-NISHI KEI-SAI: nineteenth century.

Kakémono on silk, in monochrome (A., *Cat.* p. 210, no. 663).

55. Female Sennin on Phœnix.
Painted by KAKU-DŌ: nineteenth century.

Kakémono on silk, in colours (A., *Cat.* p. 209, no. 658).

56. Chinese Lady and Monkeys.
Painted by SAKU-RAI SHIŌ-ZAN, a female artist: early nineteenth century.

Kakémono on silk, in colours (A., *Cat.* p. 241, no. 840).

The execution is in the style of the Shijō School.

57. Jigoku Reigan.
Painted by NAM-MEI: nineteenth century.

Kakémono on silk, in colours (A., *Cat.* p. 219, no. 697, *P. A. J.* pl. 41).

Reigan was a famous courtesan of the fifteenth century: the prefix Jigoku, *i.e.* Hell, is derived from her ceremonial embroidered garment here depicted.

58. Buzzard (*Butaster indicus*) on Pine-bough.
Painted by NAM-MEI: nineteenth century.

Kakémono on silk, in colours (A., *Cat.* p. 219, no. 199).

[For other examples of the Chinese School of painting in Japan, see below, Second Series, nos. 158–168.]

SESSHIŪ SCHOOL (nos. 59–61*).

The School of SESSHIŪ was one of the branches of the revived Chinese School of the fifteenth century, and its founder had the advantage of studying the parent art in its native place.

SESSHIŪ, a scion of the noble family of Ota, was born at Akabama, in the province of Bichiu, in 1421. In course of time he became a pupil of JŌSETSU, in Sōkokuji, and under his teaching acquired the manner which brings much of his work into close association with that of SHIŪBUN and certain other artists of the same period. In middle age he determined to make a voyage to China to see there the works of the old masters, and study the scenery that had inspired them. On his arrival he sought for a teacher amongst the noted artists of the time, but the men whose works were laid before him fell short of his ideal, and he resolved 'to seek instruction from the mountains, rivers, and trees of the country.' He painted many pictures during his stay, including some reminiscences of Japan, and at length his fame spread until it reached the Emperor. It is regarded as one of the most signal honours ever paid to Japanese art that SESSHIŪ received a command to paint a picture upon the wall of the Imperial palace.

After his return to Japan he lived in the temple of Unkokuji (whence the name of UNKOKU adopted by himself and many of his pupils and followers), and founded a new school from which issued many celebrated painters. He continued his work until an advanced age, and so unimpaired were his powers that some of his most valued pictures were drawn after he had numbered fourscore years. He died in 1507, at the age of eighty-six.

According to a native authority, the skill of SESSHIŪ "was the gift of nature; for he did not follow in the footsteps of the ancients, but developed a style peculiar to himself. His power was greatest in landscape, after which he excelled most in figures, then in flowers and birds; and he was also skilful in the delineation of oxen, horses, dragons, and tigers. In drawing figures and animals he completed his sketch with a single stroke of the brush, and of this style of working he is considered the originator. He preferred to paint in monochrome, and rarely made use of colours."

It is difficult for a European to estimate SESSHIŪ at his true value. His style was in its essential features the same as that of SHIŪBUN: and notwithstanding the boast of the artist that the scenery of China was his only teacher, and the credit bestowed upon him by his admirers of having invented a new style, he seems to have departed little from the artificial rules accepted by his fellow painters. He was, however, an artist of genuine power, and his renderings of Chinese scenery bear evidences of local study that we look for in vain in the works of his successors. It is in landscape that his skill is most unmistakeable.

His materials were few. He usually painted upon Chinese paper with a moderately large brush, and his drawings were either in monochrome, or strongly outlined in ink, with a few light washes of local colour. His touch was wonderfully firm, expressive, and facile, and possessed a calligraphic beauty that none but a Chinese or Japanese can thoroughly appreciate.

The two chief pupils of SESSHIŪ were SHIŪGETSU, of Satsuma, and SESSON of Hitachi; but a number of other artists of less note are recorded as having belonged to his academy during the sixteenth and seventeenth centuries.

59. Hotei and Children.
Painted by SES-SHIŪ : 1503.

> Kakémono on silk, in colours: presented to the Museum by Mr. A. W. Franks (A., *Cat.* p. 269, no. 1204).

Of the Shichifukujin, or Seven Gods of Good Fortune, Hotei (*i.e.* 'Cloth-bag,' so named from the emblem which is inseparable from him) is the most popular character, and the especial friend and playmate of children. The present picture is inscribed as having been painted by Sesshiū at the age of eighty-three.

60. Storm Dragon.
Painted by SES-SHIŪ : 1502.

> Kakémono on paper, in monochrome (A., *Cat.* p. 269, no. 1202, *P. A. J.* fig. 16).

One of a set of three pictures inscribed as having been painted by the artist at the age of eighty-two. The companion subjects, not exhibited, are a tiger, and a figure of Jurojin (one of the Seven Gods of Good Fortune).

61. Chinese Landscape.
Painted by SES-SHIŪ : fifteenth century.

> Kakémono on silk, sketched in ink and lightly tinted with colour (A., *Cat.* p. 269, no. 1205).

61*. Chinese Landscape.
Painted by SES-SHIŪ : fifteenth century.

> Screen decoration on paper, lightly tinted in colours (A., *Cat.* p. 273, no. 1228).

This is a characteristic example on a larger scale of the class of decorative landscape in imitation of the Chinese painted by the pupils of Jōsetsu. Originally used for a folding screen, and afterwards removed and rolled up, it has now been remounted and stretched across the back of the folding screen, no. 69, standing on the floor of the room.

KANO SCHOOL (nos. 62–75).

The Kano school represents the third great branch of the fifteenth-century revival of Chinese teaching in Japan. It had for

its first master a scion of the Fujiwara clan named KANO MASA-
NOBU, who was born at Odawara, in the province of Sagami, about
1424. MASANOBU is said to have studied painting under SHIŪBUN
and OGURI SŌTAN (see Chinese School), and, according to a doubtful
tradition, was at first a pupil of JŌSETSU. He seems, however, to
have exercised his skill merely as an amateur until SESSHIŪ, after
his return from China, was struck by his work and brought him
under the notice of the Shogun Yoshimasa.

He died about 1520 at the advanced age of ninety-six, leaving
two sons, OINOSUKÉ (afterwards called MOTONOBU) and UTANO-
SUKÉ (afterwards YUKINOBU). The former of these two eclipsed
his father in gifts and reputation, and must be considered the
virtual head and founder of the school. Little is known as to
MOTONOBU's early life and education, but it is said that many years
of his youth were spent in rambles through the country, with empty
purse and encumbered only by a change of clothing and the necessary implements of his craft; stopping to sketch whatever pleased
his eye; and paying his way with the produce of his brush. He
worked thus in poverty, and almost in obscurity, until between
1504 and 1521 he sent a number of his works to China, and one of
the most celebrated painters of that country was so strongly
impressed by their power that he wrote a letter to the artist, com-
paring them to the drawings of CHAO CHANG and MA YÜEN, and
expressing a wish to become his pupil. The famous metal worker
GOTŌ YŪJŌ, the Benvenuto Cellini of the age, contracted an
intimate friendship with the painter, whose designs he adopted in
the engraving of sword ornaments. His painted fans were chosen
as ceremonial gifts to the Emperor and Shōgun. Lastly, the head
of the ancient and aristocratic Tosas, MITSUSHIGÉ, thought him
worthy of the hand of his daughter, herself an artist of no small
talent; and MOTONOBU passed the remainder of a long life in great
honour and prosperity. He died at the age of eighty-two in
1559.

His most characteristic paintings, like those of SESSHIŪ, derived
little aid from mechanical finish or complexity of materials, but
were for the most part sketches either in monochrome or lightly
tinted with colour, and were dashed in with extraordinary facility,
and with a calligraphic force that has never been surpassed. All
his works display evidence of the Chinese origin of his teaching,
transmitted probably through his father from OGURI SŌTAN and
SHIŪBUN.

According to his biographers, he took for his models in landscape
the works of MA YÜEN, HIA KWEI, MUH KI, YUH KIEN, SHUN KÜ,
and TSZ' CHAO; in birds and flowers he followed CHAO CHANG, MA
YÜEN, and SHUN KÜ; his colouring was in the style of MA YÜEN,
HIA KWEI, LIANG CHI, and NGAN HWUI; and he occasionally
painted in the Japanese manner after NOBUZANÉ and TOSA MITSUNOBU.

He left three sons, and his manner of painting was preserved
with more or less modification by his younger brother UTANO-

SUKÉ, and by his earlier descendants and the adopted pupils of his line. The renown of the school lost nothing under his son SHŌYEI and his grandson YEITOKU, or under its collateral adherents SANRAKU and SANSETSU. TANYU, the fourth in descent from MOTONOBU, was one of the most vigorous and original painters of the Academy, and ranks next to the master in the estimation of the Japanese; his brothers NAONOBU and YASUNOBU were worthy associates; and, lastly, TŌUN and TSUNÉNOBU took a high position amongst the leading artists of the seventeenth century.

The works of the KANO academy exhibit two distinct manners with many intermediate gradations; the one characterised by rapidity of execution and simplicity of material, the other by decorative effect, in which full play was given for complexity of design and splendour of colouring. The first style, in which SESSHIŪ had excelled, was practised by all the KANO artists, but reached its highest perfection and greatest extravagance in the drawings of TANYU. The most 'impressionistic' of these sketches were landscapes, many of which offer an extraordinary combination of artistic treatment with a dexterity that approached dangerously near to pictorial jugglery. Such works were most frequently in monochrome, but occasionally the effect was heightened by a few light washes of colour.

The second or decorative manner was distinguished in most cases by a more careful outline, usually with a finer brush, and by a free, often lavish use of gold and colour. It was comparatively little favoured by the artists of the first three generations, but began to appear in some force in the mural embellishments of the great castles carried out in the time of Hidéyoshi by his *protégés,* YEITOKU and SANRAKU, and became more and more pronounced from the beginning of the eighteenth century, till at length all the brilliancy and elaboration of the Tosa and Buddhist paintings reappeared in the works of the school whose acknowledged masterpieces were found amongst the unobtrusive monochromes and lightly-tinted sketches of MOTONOBU and TANYU. The sharp decisive touch of the early masters, with its arbitrary variations in breadth of stroke, is, however, apparent in nearly all the works of the academy, and enables the connoisseur to distinguish specimens in which the other characteristics have been lost.

The motives favoured by the KANO artists were mostly classical —Chinese sages, Chinese landscapes, Buddhist divinities in the style of the old Chinese masters, and reproductions of the animals and flowers that had appeared in the works of the Yüen and early Ming periods—all delineated and coloured with Chinese conventionality; but Japanese subjects were by no means excluded, and occasionally the territories of other schools were trespassed upon by illustrations of ancient semi-historical stories in the Yamato-Tosa style; by humorous sketches and scenes of town life in the manner of the popular draughtsmen; and more rarely by Temple pictures on the model of the *Butsu-yé.*

62. Chung-li K'üan borne on the waves by a sword.
Painted by KA-NO MOTO-NOBU : early sixteenth century.

Kakémono on paper, in monochrome (A., *Cat.* p. 285, no. 1252, *P. A. J.* pl. 20).

Chung-li K'üan (Jap. Shōriken) is described as the first and greatest of the eight Rishi of the Tao-ists, and there are many legends concerning his miraculous birth and powers. One of his usual emblems is a sword, on which he is said to have had the power of travelling over water.

63. A Crane.
Painted by KA-NO MOTO-NOBU : early sixteenth century.

Kakémono on paper, in colours (A., *Cat.* p. 286, no. 1258).

64. Sparrow-Hawk and Quail.
Painted by KA-NO MOTO-NOBU : early sixteenth century.

Kakémono on silk, in colours (A., *Cat.* p. 286, no. 1259).

Painted with great minuteness in the style of the Yamato-Tosa school, and on a material rarely used by this artist, who worked most commonly on paper.

65. Bird on Flowering Branch.
Painted by KA-NO UTA-NO-SUKÉ : early sixteenth century.

Kakémono on paper, in colours (A., *Cat.* p. 287, no. 1266).

Kano Utanosuké was a younger brother of Kano Motonobu, and a close imitator of his manner. The bird represented is the Japanese Waxwing (*Bombycilla phœnicoptera*).

66. Mōjō Sennin.
Painted by KA-NO YEI-TOKU : sixteenth century.

Kakémono on paper, in colours (A., *Cat.* p. 288, no. 1271).

Mōjō Sennin (Chinese Mao-Nü, compare above, no. 40) is described as a wild-looking woman dressed in skins or leaves, who having been originally a maid-of-honour in the Imperial Court of China, had after the fall of the T'sin dynasty (B.C. 206) fled to the wilderness, where by fasting and contemplation she had acquired freedom from the shackles of mortality, and entered the ranks of the Rishi or Sennin.

67. Storm Dragon.
Painted by KA-NO TAN-YU : seventeenth century.

Kakémono on silk, in monochrome (A., *Cat.* p. 290, no. 1281).

One of a pair : the companion piece, not exhibited, represents a tiger. Kano Tanyu, the most celebrated artist of the school after Motonobu, was born in 1602 and died in 1674. Compare the next number.

68. Goshawk on Perch.
Painted by KA-NO TAN-YU : seventeenth century.

Kakémono on silk, .n colours (A., *Cat.* p. 290, no. 1280).

One of a pair : the companion piece, also representing a falcon, is not exhibited.

69. Chinese Landscape : with Scenes of Peasant Life.
Painted by KA-NO YASU-NOBU : seventeenth century.

Screen decoration on paper, lightly tinted in colours (A., *Cat.* p. 327, no. 1573, *P. A. J.* pl. 24).

The folding screen for which this picture was painted, and on which it is still mounted, stands on the floor of the gallery, nearly facing the other works of the Kano School. Scenes of Chinese agricultural life are very favourite subjects with the artists of the Kano School : see the following examples.

70. Rice Cultivation.
Painted by KA-NO TŌ-UN : seventeenth century.

Unmounted drawing on silk, in colours (A., *Cat.* p. 321, no. 1539).

One of a set of four scenes of Chinese life, intended for mounting as a makimono. The remaining three are not exhibited.

71. 'The Hundred Cranes.'
Painted by KA-NO MICHI-NOBU (YEI-SEN) : eighteenth century.

Portion of a makimono on silk, in colours (A., *Cat.* p. 316, no. 1445).

Two kinds of crane are here represented : the sacred crane (*Grus viridirostris*) already figured in several examples (nos. 6, 31, 63), and the white-naped crane (*Grus leuchauchen.*)

72. Chinese Landscape : with Scenes of Peasant Life.
Painted by KA-NO NAGA-NOBU (I-SEN HŌGEN) : early nine-teenth century.

Kakémono on silk, lightly tinted in colours (A., *Cat.* p. 298, no. 1337).

One of a pair : the companion piece is not exhibited.

73. Flying Squirrel (*Pteromys momoga*).
Painted by KA-NO KORÉ-NOBU : late eighteenth century.

Kakémono on silk, in colours (A., *Cat.,* p. 297, no. 1329).

74. Chinese Landscape.
Painted by KA-NO KORÉ-NOBU : late eighteenth century.

Kakémono on silk, in monochrome (A., *Cat.* p. 297, no. 1331).

One of a pair : the companion piece is not exhibited.

75. Ch'ao Yün leaping the Chasm.
Painted by KA-NO KADZŪ-NOBU : nineteenth century.

Kakémono on silk, in colours (A., *Cat.* p. 305, no. 1376).

The famous Chinese hero Ch'ao Yün (Jap. CHO-UN) was a retainer of Liu-pei, and on the defeat of his master by Ts'ao

Tsa'o in A.D. 195, took charge of and rescued his two wives and infant son. One of his adventures in the course of his escape was the leaping a huge chasm which yawned suddenly in the ground before him.

[For other examples of the Kano School, see below, Second Series, nos. 169–177.]

POPULAR SCHOOL (nos. 76–86).

The Popular School (Jap. *Ukiyo-yé Riū*) is a comparatively modern phase of Japanese art, the productions of which have been disseminated chiefly through the medium of wood-engraving. Native connoisseurs are accustomed to look down on the works of the popular artists as vulgar and trivial, in comparison with those of the classical academies of their country. But this school has had the merit of vastly extending the range and multiplying the subjects of artistic representation, as well as the good fortune of producing, in the person of the famous Hokusai, perhaps the most energetic and versatile of all the craftsmen of his race.

The motives of the school are by no means limited to the scenes of common life, but embrace all the subjects treated by its predecessors, from Buddhist divinities to caricatures. The chief subjects adopted or evolved by the new men were designs for woodcut illustrations to printed volumes of history, legend, or fiction; portraits of noted actors, wrestlers, geishas, and courtesans, mostly reproduced in coloured wood-engraving; scenes of domestic and out-door existence amongst the humbler classes; comic drawings of a new and unconventional type; native scenery, chiefly in the form of single-sheet colour-prints and illustrations to guide-books for the provinces and great cities; books of instruction in drawing, including both original sketches for imitation and also skilful reproductions of works by the old masters of China and Japan; complimentary picture-cards printed for circulation at the New Year; play-bills for the theatres; and, lastly, books of patterns for embroiderers, dyes, pipe and comb makers, and other labourers in the field of art industry.

The reputed founder of the school is one MATAHEI, a pupil of TOSA MITSUNARI, who after the close of the sixteenth century detached himself from Tosa traditions, and began to apply himself to the production of caricatures and scenes from ordinary life. But little is known of this master's work, and his example seems to have been without immediate effect. The virtual founder of the school was an artist born two generations later, HISHIGAWA MORONOBU, originally a dyer's draughtsman, who about 1680 began to publish a series of remarkably vigorous and original sketches, worthily transferred to wood by men who probably worked under the immediate direction of the artist. From this period, which may be regarded as an epoch in Japanese art, the artisan artist and the wood-engraver have laboured together with a perfect sympathy, and their joint productions may fairly claim a place apart, and one of the most prominent, in the general history of wood-engraving.

MORONOBU was the first of a long and talented line of book illustrators, amongst whom may be named OKUMURA MASANOBU, TORII KIYONOBU, TORII KIYONAGA, TACHIBANA MORIKUNI, NISHIKAWA SUKÉNOBU, TSUKIOKA TANGÉ, and KATSUGAWA SHUNSHŌ, in the eighteenth century; and ISHIDA GIOKUZAN, TAKÉHARA SHUNCHŌSAI, HOSOÏ YEISHI, KITAGAWA UTAMARO, KITAWO KEISAI MASAYOSHI, UTAGAWA TOYOHIRO, UTAGAWA TOYOKUNI, and KATSUSHIKA HOKUSAI, who worked during the opening years of the present cycle.

By the side of MORONOBU, and of equal influence with him in giving the initial impulse to the new school, was a seceder from the Kano School named HANABUSA ITCHŌ. The keenest sense of humour, observation, and enjoyment marks his drawings alike of traditional and of everyday subjects. His daring unconventionality procured his expulsion from the Kano Academy, and he was further compelled to expiate, by an eighteen years' exile to the island of Hachijo, a dangerous liberty which he ventured to take with the domestic concerns of the Shōgun in publishing the portrait of one of his female favourites amongst a series of drawings of popular beauties of the time.

MORONOBU died between 1711 and 1716, and HANABUSA ITCHŌ in 1724: and from their day onward the activity of the popular school became enormous in the production, often with inimitable skill, of every kind and variety of illustration, for wood-engraving coloured and uncoloured. A few of the chief among the many artists of the school in the eighteenth century have been mentioned above: and its efforts and powers at last reached their climax in the hands of HOKUSAI (1760–1849). Starting from the studio of the noted theatrical draughtsman KATSUGAWA SHUNSHŌ, he worked for the first half of his life at every variety of popular art, but without special recognition until the publication of the first volume of *Mangwa*, or Rough Sketches, in 1812, made him famous. The appreciation of men of letters, especially the distinguished novelist BAKIN, helping his reputation, he stood by common consent for the remainder of his life at the head of the school to which he belonged, and his is the only name of a Japanese artist at present widely known in Europe. Nourished direct from the sources of propular life and of nature, his work excels alike by the gift of dramatic insight and observation, the spirit of humour and the grotesque, a never-failing originality and energy of invention and design, and a scarcely ever surpassed power of style and hand, whether in subjects of legendary history, of popular and artisan life, of landscape, of natural history, or of pure decoration. The drawings of HOKUSAI were for the most part intended for the wood-engraver, and have been destroyed in the cutting: so that in proportion to the prodigious quantity of his

D

production, original drawings by his hand, whether in mounted or unmounted form, are rare. The same thing is true in a greater or less degree of the masters of the Popular School generally.

76. Yoshitsuné and Ladies.
Painted by HISHI-GAWA MORO-NOBU : late seventeenth century.

Kakémono on silk, in colours (A., *Cat.* p. 372, no. 1702).

Minamoto no Yoshitsuné is one of the most famous of the legendary heroes of Japan; and his exploits, with those of his gigantic adherent Benkei, are among the most frequent themes of Japanese romance and painting. He was the eighth and youngest son of Yoshitomo, who was killed in 1160 in the war against the Tairas; and half-brother of Yoritomo, the first of the Shōguns and founder of the city of Kamakura. In spite of his brilliant services against the rival Taira clan, who were at length annihilated at the battle of Yashima, he fell under the suspicions of Yoritomo, and after many cruel persecutions finally died by his own hand in 1189, at the age of thirty. He is here represented playing a flute outside a chamber in which a number of ladies are also engaged in music.

77. River Scene : with a Pleasure-barge and Bathers.
Painted by HISHI-GAWA MORO-NOBU : late seventeenth century.

Kakémono on silk, in colours (A., *Cat.* p. 372, no. 1703).

78. Holiday Amusements.
Painted by MIYA-GAWA CHŌ-SHUN : late seventeenth century.

Portion of a makimono on paper, in colours (A., *Cat.* p. 373, no. 1708).

The public flower exhibitions, and groves or avenues of cherry and other trees famous for the beauty of their blossoms, are amongst the most popular holiday resorts of the townsfolk of the great cities of Japan. Here the visitors, with cheerful faces and gaily-coloured apparel, flock in thousands, enjoying their holiday with a childish zest almost peculiar to their race. In colour and execution, the present is a singularly beautiful example of the decorative art of the popular school.

79. Geisha caressing a Cat.
Painted by JO-RAN : eighteenth century.

Kakémono on silk, in colours (A., *Cat.* p. 373, no. 1705).

80. Ébisu.
Painted by HANA-BUSA IT-CHŌ : eighteenth century.

Kakémono on paper, the fish in colour, the rest in monochrome (A., *Cat.* p. 375, no. 1721).

See above, no. 30. The god, holding his attribute, the *tai* fish, above his head, is capering gaily upon the lintel of a Shintō gateway.

81. Procession in honour of the Rice Harvest.

Painted by HANA-BUSA IT-CHŌ: eighteenth century.

Kakémono on silk, in monochrome lightly touched with colour (A., *Cat.* p. 376, no. 1725).

A number of peasants, some in white Shintō attire, are carrying a box filled with rice; others in ordinary dress are bearing torches and a staff of *go-hei*. Mount Fuji is dimly seen through the mists of nightfall.

82. A Ghost.

Painted by MAKI CHOKU-SAI: 1862.

Kakémono on silk, in colours (A., *Cat.* p. 386, no. 1764, *P. A. J.* fig. 50).

The ghost is shown floating up out of the limits of the picture: the usual brocade border being replaced by an imitation painted border of flowers (compare below, no. 118).

83. Demons trying the Bow of Tamétomo.

Painted by HOKU-SAI: 1811.

Kakémono on silk, in colours (A., *Cat.* p. 381, no. 1747, *P. A. J.* pl. 38).

Tamétomo, the grandson of Yoshiiyé, was a famous archer, whom tradition describes as of colossal stature and superhuman strength, and who lived in the latter part of the twelfth century. He is said to have visited the Isle of the Demons (Onigashima), where the trial here represented took place, to the discomfiture of the denizens of the island.

84. Jiraiya slaying the Giant Serpent.

Painter unknown: nineteenth century.

Framed picture (*gaku*) on silk, in colours (A., *Cat.* p. 400, no. 2035).

Jiraiya is the hero of a story by Kiōden, a famous novelist of the beginning of the present century. The story tells how the hero was converted from a bandit's life by the beneficent Toad Spirit, who taught him toad magic, and how to use it for the good of the people. Presently he became possessed also of the powers of snail magic, by marriage with a damsel to whom they had been imparted by the Snail Spirit. In the strength of these double powers he was able after many adventures to vanquish his rival and enemy, the great Serpent Magician. The hero is shown standing among his prostrate followers armed with a huge matchlock, while the dying serpent emits its final breath, which is seen passing in the form of a vapour across the moon. On the left appears the friendly Toad Spirit, who has been aiding in the fight, and the irregularities of the rocks are made to assume the likeness of toads. The style of the work resembles and is doubtless derived from that of Hokusai.

D 2

85. Tora watching the departure of her lover Soga no Gorō.
Painted by HIRO-SHIGÉ : nineteenth century.

Kakémono on silk, in colours (A., *Cat.* p. 383, no. 1756).

The story of the two Soga brothers, Sukénari or Jurō and Tokimuné or Gorō, and of the penalty they paid for avenging their father's death, is one of the most characteristic tales of Japanese chivalry. Tora was a courtesan of Oiso, the mistress of Gorō.

86. 'The Hundred Coolies.'
Painted by To-SHIŪ SHI-REI : nineteenth century.

Kakémono on silk, in monochrome lightly touched with colour (A., *Cat* p. 385, no. 1760).

A humorous character sketch of a crowd of coolies, some busy and some idle.

[For other examples of the Popular School, see below, Second Series, nos. 178–197].

KŌRIN SCHOOL (nos. 87–91).

The Kōrin school owes its name to OGATA KŌRIN, a famous painter and lacquer artist of the latter part of the seventeenth century. The source of KŌRIN's early education in painting is a matter of doubt. The TOSA school claims him as a pupil of SUMIYOSHI HIRO-ZUMI, while, according to another account, he was taught by KANO YASUNOBU. A third account maintains that he, his brother KENZAN, and an associate named KŌHO, had for their master a versatile artist named HONNAMI KŌYETSU (d. 1637), the grandfather of KŌHO. The works of KŌRIN present little similarity either in drawing or colouring to those of any of the established schools. They display remarkable inventive power, harmonious colouring, and usually a vigorous and expressive drawing; but in his delineations of the human figure and quadrupeds his conventionality leaves even the Tosa school far behind. His men and women have scarcely more shape or expression than indifferently-made dolls, and his horses and deer are like painted toys. His reputation rests chiefly upon his lacquer work, in which his skill was incomparable; and his influence upon industrial design in general was more strongly marked than that of any artist before the time of HOKUSAI. He died in 1716, at the age of fifty-six He is not said to have had any immediate pupils outside the lacquer industry, and it was not until the beginning of the present century that his style was revived, or anything deserving the name of a school was formed. At this time an admirer of his works named HŌITSU, a son of the Daimio Sakai Uta no Kami, and chief priest of the Nishi Hongwanji temple at Kioto, after having studied all the existing schools undertook the foundation of a new Kōrin Academy. He published three collections of the designs of KŌRIN, and himself produced many pictures in the same style. He attracted some clever pupils to the cause, and succeeded in rescuing from comparative oblivion one of the most original and characteristic of the branches of Japanese pictorial art. He is said to have died in 1828 at the age of sixty-seven.

Hōitsu was as admirable as a painter of birds, as he was extravagant in his drawings of men and women ; but he had the same graceful touch and the same instinct of harmony that reign in the works of Kōrin, and has deservedly ranked high in the estimation of his countrymen. The chief followers of the Kōrin style, after Hōitsu, were Ōho, his son; and his pupils Kiitsu, Kōson, and Kōitsu.

87. The Fording of the Tamagawa River.
Painted by O-gata Kō-rin: late seventeenth century.

Kakémono on silk, in colours (A., *Cat.* p. 407, no. 2102).

The personage on horseback fording the river is the unnamed hero (supposed to be Narihira, a poet famous for his beauty) of the *Isé Monogatari*, a Japanese novel of the tenth century. The subject is not infrequent in art, and the present example is very characteristic of its painter, alike by the empty and conventional drawing of the figures, and by the extraordinary decorative vigour, delicacy, and originality of the colour and design.

87*. White and Red Poppies.
Painted by O-gata Kō-rin: late seventeenth century.

Kakémono on silk, in colours (A., *Cat.* p. 407, no. 2101).

A floral decoration freely sketched with a full brush in a manner quite different from the preceding.

88. Cock and Chicken.
Painted by Hō-itsu: nineteenth century.

Kakémono on silk, in colours (A., *Cat.* p. 408, no. 2105).

One of a pair: the companion piece, also representing a fowl, is not exhibited.

89. Tortoises on the March.
Painted by To-nan: nineteenth century.

Unmounted drawing on paper, in monochrome (A., *Cat.* p. 411, no. 2151, *P. A. J.* pl. 60).

One of a set of twenty-three sketches similarly handled, and illustrating, with admirable dexterity of touch and truth of suggestion, the life and movements of tortoises.

90. Bamboos.
Painted by Ki-itsu: nineteenth century.

Kakémono on silk, in monochrome (A., *Cat.* p. 409, no. 2116, *P. A. J.* pl. 57).

One of a pair: the companion piece, also representing bamboos.

is not exhibited. The absence of outline, and method of rendering the roundness of the stems, is peculiar to the Kō-rin School.

91. Carp leaping a Waterfall.
Painted by KI-ITSU : nineteenth century.

Kakémono on silk, in colours (A., *Cat.* p. 408, no. 2112).

One of a pair: the companion piece, also representing a carp and waterfall, is not exhibited. This favourite subject of natural history in Japanese art is at the same time an emblem of perseverance.

SHIJŌ SCHOOL (nos. 92–118).

This is pre-eminently the naturalist school of Japan. Its founder, MARUYAMA ŌKIO, one of the most famous artists of his country, was born in the province of Tamba in 1733. After an academic art education of the usual kind, he led a reaction against the traditional practice in which he was brought up, and set up truth to nature and observation as a standard of excellence, against mere calligraphic dexterity and skill in the repetition of conventional types. Establishing himself in KIOTO, a great conservative centre, he succeeded in effecting something like a revolution in painting, and attracted to himself a number of pupils; among whom, or among their followers, are included nearly all the best animal and natural history painters, and some of the best painters of human subjects, in modern Japan. The following are the names of some of the chief representative artists of the school:—ROSETSU (died 1799), GENKI (died 1798), GEKKEI or GOSHUN, famous especially for landscapes (died 1811), NANGAKU (died 1813), MORI SOSEN (died 1821), the most brilliant animal painter of the school, famous especially for his delineations of monkeys, MORI TESSAN (died 1841), MORI IPPŌ, a pupil of TESSAN, distinguished, especially for birds, KEIBUN (died 1844), HOYEN, and lastly the great figure painter YŌSAI, who died at the age of ninety-one in 1878.

In the latter years of the last and the beginning of the present century, the influence of this school re-acted largely and beneficially on the followers of the Chinese tradition, and indeed on the schools of art in general, in Japan.

92. Carp Swimming.
Painted by MARU-YAMA Ō-KIO : 1783.

Kakémono on silk, in colours (A., *Cat.* p. 420, no. 2252).

93. Puppies at Play.
Painted by MARU-YAMA Ō-KIO : 1783.

Kakémono on silk, in colours (A., *Cat.* p. 420, no. 2255)

94. Cock in a Shower : with a Begonia in Bloom.
Painted by RAN-TOKU-SAI : 1785.
Kakémono on silk, in colours (A., *Cat.* p. 421, no. 2262, *P. A. J.* pl. 64).
Rantokusai was properly speaking a member of the Popular
school; but this example is painted, with admirable power,
in Shijō manner, and consequently classified with the works
of that school.

95. A Dream of Goblins.
Painted by MINAMOTO NO SAKI : 1778.
Portion of a makimono on paper, in colours (A., *Cat.* p. 439, no. 2366).

96. Deer and Fawn (*Cervus Shika*).
Painted by MORI SO-SEN : early nineteenth century.
Kakémono on silk, in colours (A., *Cat.* p. 425, no. 2285).
Sosen (1747–1821) was the chief animal painter of modern
Japan. This and the following are choice examples of his
highly-finished style of treatment; nos. 98 and 99 of his
contrasted rough and sketchy style.

97. Monkeys on Plum-Tree.
Painted by MORI SO-SEN : early nineteenth century.
Kakémono on silk, in colours (A., *Cat.* p. 425, no. 2283).

98. Monkeys on Tree.
Painted by MORI SO-SEN : late eighteenth century.
Kakémono on paper, in monochrome (A., *Cat.* p. 425, no. 2282).

99. Monkey.
Painted by MORI SO-SEN.
Kakémono on paper, in monochrome lightly tinted in colour (A., *Cat.* p. 424,
no. 2280).

100. Landscape ; rain scene.
Painted by ISHI-BASHI RI-CHŌ : nineteenth century.
Kakémono on silk, in monochrome (A., *Cat.* p. 226, no. 2294).
This picture is copied from the work of an earlier master of
the school, GEKKEI or GOSHUN (1742–1811).

101. 'The Cherry-Blossoms of Mikawa.'
Painted by O-TA KIN-KIN : early nineteenth century.
Kakémono on silk, in colours (A., *Cat.* p. 428, no. 2302, *P. A. J.* pl. 58).
Ota Kinkin was one of the few female artists of Japan, and
was especially in repute for her paintings of cherry-
blossoms.

102. Troop of Monkeys on Pine-tree.
Painted by HO-GEN SHIŪ-HŌ : nineteenth century.
Kakémono on silk, in colours (A., *Cat.* p. 426, no. 2291).
After Sōsen, Shiūhō was one of the most distinguished
monkey painters of Japan, and this is a favourable example
of his skill.

103. Deer grazing beside a Maple–tree ; autumn scene.
Painted by Mori Tes-san : early nineteenth century.
Kakémono on silk, in colours (A., *Cat.* p. 427, no. 2300).
Mori Tessan was a native of Osaka, and pupil of Ōkio, whose
manner, however, he adopted with modification ; he died in
1841.

104. Tiger among Rocks.
Painted by Kiu-hō Tō-yei : 1803.
Kakémono on silk, in colours (A., *Cat.* p. 438, no. 2358, *P. A. J.* pl. 66).
It is not certain whether this artist should properly be classed
under the Shijō or the Kano school. The tiger is not a
native of Japan, and though often painted by the artists of
that country, its treatment is usually traditional or imitated
from the Chinese (see nos. 119, 121, 132). The present
example has been painted from life, with some licence of
fancy in details (*e.g.* the shape of the teeth), and with a
combined power and minuteness of hand in the rendering
of the hair and coat that remind us of Albert Dürer.

105. Pea-fowl and Pine-tree.
Painted by Sai-kiō-riō Yū-sei : early nineteenth century.
Kakémono on silk, in colours (A., *Cat.* p. 430, no. 2314, *P. A. J.* pl. 33).
Though nothing is known of this painter, yet his work here
exhibited is alike by truth to nature, by vital power and
expressiveness of touch and drawing, and by imaginative
suggestion of colour, one of the most striking in the whole
collection.

106. Cuckoo flying in a Shower.
Painted by Kwan-setsu : late eighteenth century.
Kakémono on silk, in colours (A., *Cat.* p. 430, no. 2313).
A subject much affected by artists of this school (see nos.
107, 108, 109) is the flight of birds ' in the rainlight,' the
effect of rain in sky and landscape being merely suggested
in a light wash of ink, while the forms and actions of the
birds themselves are rendered with full vigour of touch, and
sometimes, as in the present instance, with considerable
finish of detail.

107. Titmice flying in a Shower.
Painted by Kei-bun: late eighteenth century.
Kakémono on silk, in colours (A., *Cat.* p. 422, no. 2265, *P. A. J.* fig. 119).
The bird represented is the Chinese titmouse (*Parus minor*).
One of a pair : for the companion piece see next number.

108. Cuckoo flying near a Waterfall.
Painted by Kei-bun: late eighteenth century.
Kakémono on silk, in colours (A., *Cat.* p. 422, no. 2266).
Companion piece to no. 107.

109. Mallards flying by Moonlight.
Painted by KEI-BUN : late eighteenth century,
Kakémono on silk, in colours (A., *Cat.* p. 422, no. 2268).
The birds represented are a male and female mallard (*Anas boschas*).

110. Hadésu killing the Korean Tiger.
Painted by YŌ-SAI : nineteenth century.
Kakémono on silk, in colours (A., *Cat.* p. 435, no. 2345, *P. A. J.*, pl. 34).
Kikuchi Yōsai, named also Takéyasu, was one of the most gifted artists of his age, and died at ninety-one in 1878. Unlike most painters of his school, he devoted himself chiefly to figure subjects, and his chief work was the series of portraits of Japanese celebrities designed and engraved for the book called *Zenken Kojitsu.*—The story of Hadésu is as follows :—Kashiwa-déno Omi Hadésu was sent, accompanied by his family, as ambassador from the Emperor Kimmei to Korea, in A.D. 545. One snowy night during his stay in that country his little daughter was lost. Search was vain, until at last a bloody track marked by the footprints of a tiger gave a clue to the mystery, and the father determined to follow the beast to its lair. The tiger was on the alert, and came towards him with open mouth, but Hadésu, thrusting his hand between its jaws, seized the creature's tongue and plunged a sword into its body.

111. The Grasshopper Procession.
Painted by HO-YEN : early nineteenth century.
Kakémono on silk, in colours (A., *Cat.* p. 422, no. 2264).
The feudal procession of a Daimio burlesqued by insects ; compare above, no. 44. Hoyen was one of the most graceful and influential painters of animal and vegetable life of his school and century. For other drawings by him and by his scholars see below, Second Series, nos. 205–222.

112. Pea-fowl and Peonies.
Painted by KŌ-SEI : nineteenth century.
Kakémono on silk, in monochrome, touched with gold (A., *Cat.* p. 431, no. 2318).

113. A Roadside Robbery in Winter.
Painter unknown : nineteenth century.
Kakémono on silk, in colours (A., *Cat.* p. 436, no. 2351).

114, 115. Landscapes, a pair : Spring and Autumn.
Painted by MORI IP-PŌ : nineteenth century.
Kakémonos on silk, in colours (A., *Cat.* p. 423, nos. 2272, 2272A).

116. Cranes Flying.
Painted by MORI IP-PŌ : nineteenth century.
Kakémono on silk, in colours (A., *Cat.* p. 423, no. 2275, *P. A. J.* pl. 62).
A masterpiece of the artist and the school.

117. Peacock on Pine-bough.

Painted by MORI IP-PŌ : nineteenth century.

Kakémono on silk, in colours (A., *Cat.* p. 423, no. 2273).

118. Chung Kwei and the Demons.

Painted by SHIBA-TA ZÉ-SHIN : nineteenth century.

Kakémono on silk, in colours (A., *Cat.* p. 437, no. 2355, *P. A. J.* pl. 45).

The demons are represented as kicked down by the hero out
of the limits of the picture : the usual brocade border being
replaced by an imitation painted border (compare above,
no. 82). Chung Kwei (Jap. Shōki), the Demon-queller, is
a popular personage of Chinese, and by adoption of Japanese,
mythology. In the reign of the Emperor Kao Tsu (Jap.
Kōso), 618–627 A.D., having failed to attain the position to
which he aspired in the State examination, he killed himself for shame, but at his burial was raised by imperial
command to posthumous honours—in requital for which
favour his spirit undertook the office of a kind of ghostly
protector to a subsequent Emperor, Ming Hwang (Jap.
Gensō, A.D. 713–762), when his palace was haunted by
demons.

[For other examples of the Shijō School, see below, Second
Series, nos. 198–273.]

GANKU SCHOOL (nos. 119–133).

This is the youngest of the recognised art schools or academies
of Japan. Its founder, KISHI DŌKŌ, better known by his *nom de
pinceau* of GANKU, was born in Kanazawa, in the province of Kaga,
about the middle of the last century. He was at first a retainer
of Prince Arisugawa, subsequently entering the service of the
Emperor, and appears to have originally adopted painting as an
amusement; but in his later years the pursuit became a profession,
and gave him a high position amongst the art teachers of Kioto.
His style was based upon the pictures of the old Chinese masters
of the Sung Dynasty, but by importations from various other
sources underwent sufficient modification to give to his work a
distinctive character, which can also be recognized in that of his
pupils. He was especially noted for his drawings of tigers, in
which he was a close imitator of the Sung artists, but his delineations of birds indicate that the fame of ŌKIO's teaching had not
been without an effect upon his theories. The naturalistic element
was, however, far less apparent in his works than in those of some
of his pupils, who approached so closely to the Shijō practice that
the separation of the paintings of the two academies is often
a task of some difficulty. He died in 1838, at the age of 89.

Among his principal followers were his eldest son GANTAI
(died 1863), his nephew GANRIŌ, especially noted for drawings of
flowers and insects, his son-in-law RENZAN or GANTOKU (died 1859),
whose manner closely approaches that of the Shijō School; with

BUMPŌ, TEMMIN, CHIKUDŌ, and lastly BUNRIN, (died 1877), one of the most refined and original of the modern landscape-painters of Japan.

119. Tiger at Rest.
Painted by GAN-KU: early nineteenth century.

Kakémono on silk, in monochrome lightly touched with colour (A., *Cat.* p. 452, no. 2702).

120. Monkeys.
Painted by GAN-KU and GAN-TAI: early nineteenth century.

Kakémono on silk, in ink, slightly touched with colour (A., *Cat.* p. 452, no. 2707).

121. Tiger and Bamboos, in Rain.
Painted by GAN-TAI: nineteenth century.

Kakémono on silk, in monochrome (A., *Cat.* p. 454, no. 2710, *P. A. J.* pl. 67).

122. Spring View of Mount Fuji.
Painted by GAN-TAI: nineteenth century.

Kakémono on silk, lightly tinted in colours (A., *Cat.* p. 454, no. 2711).

123, 124. Chinese Landscapes, with Figures: a Pair.
Painted by GAN-TOKU (REN-ZAN): nineteenth century.

Kakémonos on silk, lightly tinted in colours (A., *Cat.* p. 454, nos. 2713, 2712).

125. View of Lake Biwa by Moonlight.
Painted by BUN-RIN: nineteenth century.

Framed drawing on silk, in monochrome (A., *Cat.* p. 451, no. 2728, *P. A. J.* pl. 55).

126. Morning Mists on the Yodo River.
Painted by BUN-RIN: nineteenth century.

Unmounted drawing on silk, lightly tinted in colours (A., *Cat.* p. 456, no. 2726, *P. A. J.* pl. 51).

One of a pair: see next number.

127. Moonlight Scene near Kioto.
Painted by BUN-RIN: nineteenth century.

Kakémono on silk, lightly tinted in colours (A., *Cat.* p. 455, no. 2727).

Companion piece to the above.

128. Sparrow and Peony.
Painted by BUN-RIN: nineteenth century.

Kakémono on silk, in colours (A., *Cat.* p. 454, no. 2721).

129. Sparrows flying in a Shower.
Painted by CHIKU-DŌ: nineteenth century.

Kakémono on silk, in colours (A., *Cat.* p. 455, no. 2718).

Painted in the style of the Shijō school: the bird represented in this and the above examples is again the Tree Sparrow (*Passer montanus*).

130. Monkeys and Grass.
Painted by CHIKU-DŌ: nineteenth century.

Kakémono on silk, in colours (A., *Cat.* p. 455, no. 2719).

131. Peasant and Wife resting under a Gourd.
Painted by KWA-ZAN: nineteenth century.

Kakémono on silk, in colours (A., *Cat.* p. 437, no. 2724).

MIXED SCHOOL (nos. 132–133).

132. Tiger on the Spring.
Painted by I-KO: early nineteenth century.

Kakémono on silk, in monochrome (A., *Cut.* p. 208, no. 649).

One of a pair: the companion piece, representing a dragon, is not exhibited.

133. The Thousand Carp.
Painted by I-KO: early nineteenth century.

Kakémono on silk, in monochrome and gold (A., *Cut.* p. 240, no. 818, *P. A. J.* pl. 59).

The spectator is supposed to be looking into the water, as through the glass front of an aquarium, at an approaching shoal of carp. The painting in many respects contradicts the ordinary practice of Sinico-Japanese Art, in comprising a careful observance of the laws of apparent size in ratio to distance, and an almost scientific conception of high lights and shadow gradations. The style of colouring is that of the Chinese school, but the design is more suggestive of Shijō teaching. The use of gold to render the effect of high lights is worthy of remark.

Very little is known of the painter of these last two kakémonos, who is reputed to have been an amateur practising about the end of the last and the beginning of the present century, and who evidently adopted eclectic principles of design.

SECOND SERIES.

The drawings exhibited in this series are placed in the show-cases on the floor of the Room. The numbers begin at the north-east corner farthest from the entrance, and proceed from left to right,. ending with the case nearest to the Ceramic Gallery (see Plan).

YAMATO-TOSA SCHOOL (nos. 134–157).

[For other examples of this School, see above, First Series, nos. 20–33.]

The following set of Drawings, arranged in the first two· show-cases (beginning as above mentioned), illustrate one of the most familiar of Japanese tales, that of the destruction of the Shiuten Dōji, a ravening ogre or demon, by the hero Minamoto no Yorimitsu, better known as Raikō. The date given to this exploit in chronological works is A.D. 947. The tenor of the story, which is closely analogous to that of similar tales in the West, will be clear from the episodes here illustrated. The explanation of the several scenes is as follows :—

134. Story of Raikō and the Shiuten Dōji.
Painter unknown : seventeenth century.

Raikō receives the Imperial commission to exterminate the ogre and his demons.

135. Story of Raikō and the Shiuten Dōji.
Painter unknown : seventeenth century.

Preparations for departure. Council of Raikō with his six squires. The inferior retainers are sharpening the swords,. preparing food for the journey, and feeding the horses.

136. Story of Raikō and the Shiuten Dōji.
Painter unknown : seventeenth century.

The departure. The band have adopted the disguise of peripatetic Buddhist priests, and are utilising as receptacles· for their armour the portable wooden cases which the priests are accustomed to carry on their backs.

137. Story of Raikō and the Shiuten Dōji.
Painter unknown : seventeenth century.

Journey through the mountains. The hero and his band

encounter a friendly spirit, the spirit of Sumiyoshi, who
appears in the form of a venerable old man.

138. Story of Raikō and the Shiuten Dōji.
Painter unknown : seventeenth century.

The friendly Spirit entertains the party, and is served with
marks of profound respect by Raikō himself. He presents
Raikō with a close-fitting helmet to wear beneath his own,
and a poisonous drug to be used for the purpose of stupefy-
ing the monster.

139. Story of Raikō and the Shiuten Dōji.
Painter unknown : seventeenth century.

Raikō and his band, under the guidance of the friendly Spirit,
continue their journey and are seen crossing a tree bridge.

140. Story of Raikō and the Shiuten Dōji.
Painter unknown : seventeenth century.

Raikō and his band arrive under the guidance of the Spirit at
the borders of a mountain lake.

141. Story of Raikō and the Shiuten Dōji.
Painter unknown : seventeenth century.

Raikō and his band discover a weeping lady washing a bloody
garment in a stream. She directs the travellers to the
home of the monster.

142. Story of Raikō and the Shiuten Dōji.
Painter unknown : seventeenth century.

Raikō and his band arrive at the gates of the ogre's castle,
and receive an ironical welcome from his demon guards.

143. Story of Raikō and the Shiuten Dōji.
Painter unknown : seventeenth century.

Raikō and his band are entertained by the ogre, who receives
them in one of the various forms he has the power to assume : viz., that of a huge and bloated boy in Chinese garb.
The newly-severed leg of a woman is set before the guests.
Raikō eats with seeming relish while his comrades look on
with stolid countenances.

144. Story of Raikō and the Shiuten Dōji.
Painter unknown : seventeenth century.

The adventurers prepare saké for their host, who is now
attended by two richly-dressed ladies. It is shown how
the liquor is being secretly tempered with the drug received
from the Spirit of Sumiyoshi.

145. Story of Raikō and the Shiuten Dōji.
Painter unknown: seventeenth century.

The Orgie. The Shiuten Dōji is succumbing to the influence of the drink. A demon performs a comic dance which is greatly applauded by his comrades and the heroes.

146. Story of Raikō and the Shiuten Dōji.
Painter unknown: seventeenth century.

The Ogre has been carried off to his sleeping quarters overcome with drink. His demon guards are seen succumbing to the same influence, as the heroes continue to ply them with the drugged liquor.

147. Story of Raikō and the Shiuten Dōji.
Painter unknown: seventecuth century.

The heroes take counsel with the captive ladies.

148. Story of Raikō and the Shiuten Dōji.
Painter unknown: seventeenth century.

The heroes arm for the attack.

149. Story of Raikō and the Shiuten Dōji.
Painter unknown; seventeenth century.

The heroes are secretly conducted by the captive ladies towards the sleeping apartments of the Ogre.

150. Story of Raikō and the Shiuten Dōji.
Painter unknown: seventeenth century.

The Ogre's chamber. To the right appear the heroes outside. about to push open the sliding doors, while the friendly Spirit hands them a coil of magic rope. To the left is the interior of the room, where the Shiuten Dōji, resuming his true form in sleep, is seen as a hideous flame-coloured demon lying in a state of drunken stupor. A number of fair captives soothe him to sleep by stroking his limbs. Some of the ladies make signs that their deliverers are at hand.

151. Story of Raikō and the Shiuten Dōji.
Painter unknown: seventeenth century.

The attack. The giant, having been bound during his sleep to the pillars of the apartment, has been decapitated by a stroke of Raikō's sabre. The writhing trunk and members have snapped all the bonds save one—presumably that brought by the Spirit of Sumiyoshi—while the severed head, after springing high into the air, has darted down on Raikō like a beast of prey, seizing his helmet with its fangs. Raikō falls on one knee, but is saved by the under cap of steel, the gift of the friendly Spirit. In the meantime the

knights hack at the struggling frame on the floor, while
the ladies fly in terror from the scene.

152. Story of Raikō and the Shiuten Dōji.
Painter unknown : seventeenth century.

The charnel house. The knights, under the guidance of three
of the ladies, have reached the den which is the Ogre's
shambles and larder.

153. Story of Raikō and the Shiuten Dōji.
Painter unknown : seventeenth century.

The heroes capture two of the demon guardians of the
shambles.

154. Story of Raikō and the Shiuten Dōji.
Painter unknown : seventeenth century.

The heroes execute the captured guards.

155. Story of Raikō and the Shiuten Dōji.
Painter unknown : seventeenth century.

The heroes return through the mountain passes in company
with the rescued ladies.

156, 157. Story of Raikō and the Shiuten Dōji.
Painter unknown : seventeenth century.

Raikō and his band return in triumph, accompanied by the
spoils of their expedition, between files of high-born spec-
tators, to the presence of the Mikado, which is indicated by
the wheels of his sacred ox-chariot.

The above nos., 134–157, are selected from a set of thirty-four unmounted
drawings on paper, in colours, intended for mounting as a makimono, by
an unknown painter of the Yamato-Tosa school in the seventeenth century
(A., *Cat.* pp. 146–150, nos. 383–416).

The special characteristics of the workmanship, such as the
precise and minute drawing of features and extremities,
in a manner not much unlike that of Persian miniature-
painting, the extreme care in all points of accessory,
costume, and furniture, the conventional cast of countenance
and attitude in the women, the use of a uniform pattern of
highly-conventionalized cloud, the vivid and rather harsh
colouring, especially in the greens, with the dramatic and
effective manner of setting forth the story, are all eminently
characteristic of the later work of the school.

CHINESE SCHOOL (nos. 158–168).

[For other examples of this school, see above, First Series,
nos. 34–58.]

158. Sparrows and Hibiscus.
Painter unknown : 1657.

159. Painted Snipe (*Rhynchea capensis*) and St. John's Wort.
Painter unknown : 1657.

160. Cormorant (*Phalacrocorax capillatus*) on Rock.
Painter unknown : 1657.

161. Kingfisher (*Alcedo bengalensis*) and Bittern.
Painter unknown : 1657.

162. Duck and Iris.
Painter unknown : 1657.

163. Cuckoo and flowering Shrub.
Painter unknown : 1657.

164. Bird and Lily.
Painter unknown : 1657.

165. Flycatcher (*Muscicapa narcissina*) and Hibiscus.

166. Golden Pheasant (*Phasianus pictus*) and St. John's Wort.
Painter unknown : 1657.

The above nos., 158-165, are selected from a set of thirty-eight coloured sketches on paper by an unknown Japanese artist of the Chinese school, dating in the third year of Meirekei, = 1657 (A., *Cat.* p. 261, nos. 1089-1126).

167. Wagtail (*Motacilla japonica*) and Dead Leaves.
Painted by SA-TAKÉ YEI-KAI : nineteenth century.

Fan-mount on silk, in colours (A., *Cat.* p. 252, no. 951).

168. Rats stealing Eggs.
Painted by SA-TAKÉ YEI-KAI : nineteenth century.

Fan-mount on silk, monochrome, lightly touched with colour (A., *Cat.* p. 252, no. 952, *P. A. J.* fig. 53).

KANO SCHOOL (nos. 169-177).

[For other examples of this school, see above, First Series, nos. 62-71.]

169. Design for a Saddle : Birds and Water.
Painted by KA-NO YŪ-HO : eighteenth century.

170. Design for a Saddle : Shells and Seaweed.
Painted by KA-NO YŪ-HO : eighteenth century.

171. Design for a Saddle : Wild Geese and Rushes.
Painted by KA-NO YŪ-HO : eighteenth century.

172. Design for a Saddle : Leaves, Ferns, and Cord.
Painted by KA-NO YŪ-HO : eighteenth century.

173. Design for a Saddle : Chrysanthemums.
Painted by KA-NO YŪ-HO : eighteenth century.

E

174. Design for a Saddle : a flowering Tree.
Painted by KA-NO YŪ-HO: eighteenth century.

175. Design for a Saddle : a Rice-field.
Painted by KA-NO YŪ-HO: eighteenth century.

176. Design for a Saddle : Butterflies.
Painted by KA-NO YŪ-HO: eighteenth century.

177. Design for a Saddle : Millet.
The above nos., 169–177, are selected from a set of twenty-five designs for lacquered saddle-fronts, on paper, in colours (A., *Cat.* p. 317, nos. 1480–1504).

POPULAR SCHOOL (nos. 178–197).

[For other examples of this school, see above, First Series, nos. 76–84.]

178. Bird and Convolvulus.
Painted by HOKU-SAI: nineteenth century.
Drawing on silk, in colours (A., *Cat.* p. 398, no. 1899).

---

179. Kusunoki Masashigé and his Son.
Painted by HOKU-SAI: nineteenth century.

Kusunoki Masashigé is one of the most famous examples of courage and loyalty in Japanese history. In 1331 he was designated by the Emperor to defend the cause of the throne against the rebel Takatoki. A few years later, in 1336, he was pitted against a more formidable foe in Ashikaga Takauji. Again he won a victory for the Imperial forces, and suggested a scheme for wholly crushing the Ashikagas, but his advice being rejected, he precipitated himself into an unequal conflict against a large army under Takauji. Nearly all his retainers died fighting around him, and at last, the day lost, he retired with his brother, the survivors of his staff, and sixty followers, to a farmer's house in Minatogawa, where the whole number committed suicide. Before ending his life, the hero called his eldest son before him and gave him (in the manner here depicted) the ancestral roll as a precious heirloom to stimulate him to deeds of heroism.

180. Racoon-faced Dog in disguise.
Painted by HOKU-SAI: nineteenth century.

The racoon-faced dog (Tanuki) is in Japan the subject of as many legends, and credited with as great powers of transformation and mischief, as the fox. He is here represented dressed as a priest, and examining a trap baited with a dead rat.

181. **Rats and capsicum Pods.**
Painted by HOKU-SAI : nineteenth century.

182. **Cray-fish, Orange, Fern-frond, &c.**
Painted by HOKU-SAI : nineteenth century.
A New Year's symbolical decoration.

183. **Frog swimming.**
Painted by HOKU-SAI : nineteenth century.
The above five numbers, 179–183, form a series of drawings on silk, in colours.
(A., *Cat.* p. 379, nos. 1772–1776).

184. **Snakes, Newts, Frogs, Locusts, Bees, &c.**
Painted by TŌ-TEI HOKU-SHI : nineteenth century.

185. **Ladies with a Birdcage : and other Figures.**
Painted by TŌ-TEI HOKU-SHI : nineteenth century.

186. **Scene from a Novel.**
Painted by TŌ-TEI HOKU-SHI : nineteenth century.
The above three numbers are drawings on paper, 184 in colours, 185 and 186 in monochrome, selected from a set of thirty sheets of miscellaneous sketches by the same artist (A., *Cat.* p. 390, nos. 1779–1816).

TŌTEI HOKUSHI was a pupil and imitator of HOKUSAI, and his close relation to his master is especially to be discerned in the sheet of natural history studies, no. 184.

187. **Japanese Landscape.**
Painted by HIRO-SHIGÉ : nineteenth century.
Drawing on silk, in colours (A., *Cat.* p. 397, no. 1895).
One of a pair; the companion piece is not exhibited.

188. **Carp.**
Painted by UTA-GAWA TOKO-YUNI the Second : nineteenth century.
Drawing on silk, in monochrome (A., *Cat.* p. 394, no. 1826).
In the style of the Shijō School; compare First Series, no. 92.

189. **Turning the Tables : Snake triumphed over by Frogs.**
Painted by KIŌ-SAI : 1879.

190. **Turning the Tables : Snake crucified by Frogs.**
Painted by KIŌ-SAI : 1879.

191. Tortoises and other animals : an Execution Scene.
Painted by Kiŏ-sai : 1879.

Two tortoises are already hanged by the neck, while a third,
suspended by the tail, serves as a target to the arrows of a
troop of monkeys, frogs, and brother tortoises; below on the
right the mythical Kappa is seen gesticulating.

**192. Turning the Tables : a Cat captured and tormented
by Rats.**
Painted by Kiŏ-sai : 1879.

**193. Turning the Tables : a Man dragged in bonds by
Wolves, Hares, &c.**
Painted by Kiŏ-sai : 1879.

194. Men chased by Wolves.
Painted by Kiŏ-sai : 1879.

The above six numbers, 189–194, are selected from a set of forty-five
burlesque drawings on paper, in colours (A., *Cat.* p. 395, nos. 1847–1891).

**195. A Sinner after Death brought before Yama, King of
Hell.**
Painted by Kiŏ-sai : 1879.

**196. Yama, King of Hell, presiding at the punishment of
Sinners.**
Painted by Kiŏ-sai : 1879.

197. The Punishment of Sinners.
Painted by Kiŏ-sai : 1879.

The above three numbers, 195–197, are selected from a set of five burlesque
drawings on paper, in colours (A., *Cat.* p. 394, nos. 1827–1831).

The painter of the two series from which the above examples
are taken, Kawanabé Kiŏsai, was born in 1831, and is still
living. He is one of the most vigorous pupils of the school
of Hoku-sai, and in the burlesque vein especially, an artist
of great originality and fertility; though the evidences of
carelessness often mar the quality of his work.

SHIJŌ SCHOOL (nos. 198–273).

[For other examples of this school, see above, First Series,
nos. 92–118.]

198. The Seven Calamities : the Great Serpent.
Painted by Minamoto no Ō-kŏ, after Ō-kio : 1773.

199. The Seven Calamities : the Great Bird.
Painted by Minamoto no Ō-kŏ, after Ō-kio : 1773.

200. The Seven Calamities: Lightning.
Painted by MINAMOTO NO Ō-KŌ, after Ō-KIO: 1773.

201. The Seven Calamities: Earthquake.
Painted by MINAMOTO NO Ō-KŌ, after Ō-KIO: 1773.

202. The Seven Calamities: Hurricane.
Painted by MINAMOTO NO Ō-KŌ, after Ō-KIO: 1773.

203. The Seven Calamities: Inundation.
Painted by MINAMOTO NO Ō-KŌ, after Ō-KIO: 1773.

204. The Seven Calamities: Gateway of the Mikado's Palace.
Painted by MINAMOTO NO Ō-KŌ, after Ō-KIO: 1773.

It is not easy to understand the connection of this peaceful scene which closes the Series of the Seven Calamities, with the scenes of horror which precede it. It may perhaps be introduced only by way of contrast.

The above seven numbers, 198-204, constitute a complete series of drawings on silk, in colours (A., *Cat.* p. 444, nos. 2631-2637).

---

205. Plum-branch.
Painted by HO-YEN: nineteenth century.

[For another work of this master, see above, First Series, no. 111.]

206. Sparrow on Plum-branch.
Painted by NAN-REI: nineteenth century.

207. Melon.
Painted by KIŌ-HO: nineteenth century.

208. St. John's Wort.
Painted by NAN-REI: nineteenth century.

209. Blue-backed Flycatcher (*Muscicapa cyanomelana*) and Hibiscus.
Painted by KŌ-YŌ: nineteenth century.

210. Water-Lily.
Painted by KAN-YEI: nineteenth century.

211. Dead Fish and Bamboo.
Painted by SHI-ZAN: nineteenth century.

212. Tortoise and Water-plant.
Painted by RIŌ-SETSU: nineteenth century.

213. Carp swimming.
Painted by KIN-REI: nineteenth century.

214. Lychnis in Flower.
Painted by GIOKU-AN: nineteenth century.

215. White–flowering Pomegranate.
Painted by Go-SEN : nineteenth century.

216. Cicada and Pine–bough.
Painted by SHUN-KŌ: nineteenth century.

217. Boys Fishing.
Painted by Kŏ-YŎ: nineteenth century.

[For other paintings by this master, see below, nos. 243–259.]

218. Scroll Genius.
Painted by Kŏ-SAN: nineteenth century.

219. A Samurai in Armour.
Painted by SHŎ-GAKU: nineteenth century.

220. Fisherman with Net.
Painted by BAI-SHŎ: nineteenth century.

221. Chinese Boys with a Book.
Painted by Go-SEN: nineteenth century.

222. Liu Pei plunging into the Stream.
Painted by KISU-I: nineteenth century.

Liu Pei (Jap. Riubi or Gentoku) historically known as Chao
Lieh Ti, was a famous soldier of fortune of the 3rd century
A.D., who rose from the position of a vendor of straw shoes
to the throne of one of the three kingdoms into which China
was divided after the fall of the Han Dynasty. He died
A.D. 222, shortly after his accession to sovereign power.
The story relating to the incident here depicted has not yet
been traced.

The above eighteen numbers, 205–222, belong to a series of nineteen drawings on silk, in colours, by HOYEN and various of his scholars (A., *Cat.*
p. 440, nos. 2377–2395).

223. Japanese Spotted Kingfisher (*Coryle lugubris*).
Painted by No-DA Tŏ-MIN: early nineteenth century.

224. Domestic Hen.
Painted by No-DA Tŏ-MIN: early nineteenth century.

225. Garganey (*Anas circea*).
Painted by No-DA Tŏ-MIN: early nineteenth century.

226. Little Grebes (*Podiceps minor*).
Painted by No-DA Tŏ-MIN: early nineteenth century.

227. Mandarin Duck and Drake (*Anas galericulata*).
Painted by No-DA Tŏ-MIN: early nineteenth century.

228. Mandarin Duck and Drake (*Anas galericulata*).
Painted by No-DA Tŏ-MIN: early nineteenth century.

229. Teal (*Anas crecca*).
Painted by No-DA Tō-MIN: early nineteenth century.

230. Female Teal, female Shoveller (*Anas clypeata*), and **Moorhen** (*Gallinula chloropus*).
Painted by No-DA Tō-MIN: early nineteenth century.

231. Woodcock (*Scolopax rusticola*).
Painted by No-DA Tō-MIN: early nineteenth century.

232. Siberian Water-Rails (*Rallus indicus*).
Painted by No-DA Tō-MIN: early nineteenth century.

233. Red-eared Bulbul (*Hypsipetes amaurotis*), **Dove**, and **Young Starling.**
Painted by No-DA Tō-MIN: early nineteenth century.

234. Dove and Cuckoo.
Painted by No-DA Tō-MIN: early nineteenth century.

235. White's Thrush (*Geocichla varia*), **Rock Thrush** (*Monticola saxatilis*) and **Tree Sparrow** (*Passer montanus*).
Painted by No-DA Tō-MIN: early nineteenth century.

236. Japanese Jay (*Garrulus japonicus*).
Painted by No-DA Tō-MIN: early nineteenth century.

237. Silver Pheasant (*Euplocamus nycthemerus*).
Painted by No-DA Tō-MIN: early nineteenth century.

238. Domestic Cock.
Painted by No-DA Tō-MIN: early nineteenth century.

239. Widgeon (?), **with a Mandarin Drake and Duck lightly sketched.**
Painted by No-DA Tō-MIN: early nineteenth century.

240. Formosan Heron (*Butorides macrorhynchus*).
Painted by No-DA Tō-MIN: early nineteenth century.

241. Heron and Pochard (?).
Painted by No-DA Tō-MIN: early nineteenth century.

242. White Ducks (? Dusky Mallard, *Anas zonorhyncha*).
Painted by No-DA Tō-MIN: early nineteenth century.

The above nineteen numbers, 223–242, are selected from a series of forty-six sketches on paper, in colours, by the same artist (A., *Cat.* p. 444, nos. 2447–2492).

---

243. Rice-bird (*Padda oryzivora*) **on Plum-branch.**
Painted by Kō-Yō: nineteenth century.

244. Goldcrests (*Regulus cristatus japonicus*) and **Maple-branch.**
Painted by Kō-Yō: nineteenth century.

245. Wren (*Troglodytes parvus fumigatus*) **and Narcissus.**
Painted by Kō-yō: nineteenth century.

246. ? Japanese Knot (*Tringa crassirostris*) **and Iris.**
Painted by Kō-yō : nineteenth century.

247. Cuckoo, Nut-branch, and Crescent Moon.
Painted by Kō-yō: nineteenth century.

248. Japanese Titmouse (*Parus varius*) **and Convolvulus.**
Painted by Kō-yō: nineteenth century.

249. Sparrow (*Passer montanus*) **and Desmodeum.**
Painted by Kō-yō: nineteenth century.

250. Chinese Great Titmouse (*Parus minor*) **and Chrysanthemum.**
Painted by Kō-yō : nineteenth century.

251. Chinese Golden-wing (*Fringilla sinica*) **on wild Cherry-bough.**
Painted by Kō-yō: nineteenth century.

252 ? American Pipit (*Anthus ludovicianus*) **and Valerian.**
Painted by Kō-yō : nineteenth century.

253. Indian Kingfisher (*Alcedo ispida bengalensis*) **and Water-plant.**
Painted by Kō-yō: nineteenth century.

254. Red-billed Magpie (*Urocissa sinensis*) **on Pomegranate-branch.**
Painted by Kō-yō : nineteenth century.

255. Eastern Turtle–Dove (*Turtur gelastes*) **and Commelina.**
Painted by Kō-yō: nineteenth century.

256. Mallards.
Painted by Kō-yō: nineteenth century.

257. Bull–headed Shrike (*Lanius bucephalus*) **on Nut–bough.**
Painted by Kō-yō: nineteenth century.

258. Masked Bunting (*Emberiza personata*) **on Magnolia-bough.**
Painted by Kō-yō: nineteenth century.

259. Japanese Green Woodpecker (*Gesinus awokera*) **on Pine-tree.**
Painted by Kō-yō: nineteenth century.

The above seventeen numbers, 243–259, are selected from a series of twenty-one sketches on paper, in colours, by the same artist (A., *Cat.* p. 441, nos. 2396–2416).

260. Mallards flying in Snow.
Painted by SHŌ-SHŌ-TO KAGÉ-MURA : nineteenth century.

261. Grasshoppers on flowering Shrub : Moonlight.
Painted by SHŌ-SHŌ-TO KAGÉ-MURA : nineteenth century.

262. Sparrows and Mulberry : a Shower.
Painted by SHŌ-SHŌ-TO KAGÉ-MURA : nineteenth century.

263. Fire-flies, Grasses, and Convolvulus.
Painted by SHŌ-SHŌ-TO KAGÉ-MURA : nineteenth century.

264. White-naped Cranes (*Grus leuchauchen*).
Painted by SHŌ-SHŌ-TO KAGÉ-MURA : nineteenth century.

The above five numbers, 260-264, form a series of delicately executed drawings on silk, in colours (A., *Cat.* p. 441, nos. 2417-2421).

265. Quail (*Coturnix communis*).
Painter unknown : nineteenth century.

266. Buntings (*Emberiza rustica*).
Painter unknown : nineteenth century.

267. Quail (*Coturnix communis*).
Painter unknown : nineteenth century.

268. Japanese Titmouse (*Parus varius*).
Painter unknown : nineteenth century.

269. Dove.
Painter unknown : nineteenth century.

270. Flycatcher.
Painter unknown : nineteenth century.

271. Tree Sparrow (*Passer montanus*).
Painter unknown : nineteenth century.

272. Silk Starling (*Sturnus sericus*).
Painter unknown : nineteenth century.

273. Japanese Titmouse (*Parus varius*).
Painter unknown : nineteenth century.

The above nine numbers, 265-273, are selected from a set of thirty carefully finished drawings on paper, in colours, by the same unknown artist (A., *Cat.* p. 444, nos. 2493-2522).

THE END.

F

www.ingramcontent.com/pod-product-compliance
Lightning Source LLC
Chambersburg PA
CBHW021632270326
41931CB00008B/979

* 9 7 8 3 3 3 7 1 6 4 1 2 6 *